on track ...

The Byrds

every album, every song

Andy McArthur

SONIC**BOND**

sonicbondpublishing.com

Sonicbond Publishing Limited
www.sonicbondpublishing.co.uk
Email: info@sonicbondpublishing.co.uk

First Published in the United Kingdom 2023
First Published in the United States 2023

British Library Cataloguing in Publication Data:
A Catalogue record for this book is available from the British Library

Copyright Andy McArthur 2023

ISBN 978-1-78952-280-8

Typeset in ITC Garamond & ITC Avant Garde
Printed and bound in England

Graphic design and typesetting: Full Moon Media

Follow us on social media:
Twitter: https://twitter.com/SonicbondP
Instagram: https://www.instagram.com/sonicbondpublishing_/
Facebook: https://www.facebook.com/SonicbondPublishing/

Linktree QR code:

Acknowledgements

Eternal thanks go to my wife Karen and daughters Amy and Zoe for putting up with me while writing the book. A huge thanks also go to 'my drummers' Jim and Bob for their continuous help (and beers), and to Dave, John and Martin for their advice. Gratitudes also to Tony and Michael for their top-10s and comments, and to 'Watty' and Mr. Livingston – my friend and teacher – for making my first BASF tape of the Byrds in 1982! Life has never been the same since.

I'd also like to express gratitude to David Wells at Grapefruit Records, music journalist Barney Hoskyns, author Richie Unterberger, and musician and writer Sid Griffin for their opinions and insight. Special thanks go to Martin Orkin – author of the book *Rivals of the Beatles* – who was always gracious and generous with his opinions and advice, and whose kind words lifted my spirits as deadlines loomed. Immense thanks also to Stephen at Sonicbond for allowing me the chance to write my book, and for all his help and guidance.

I would also like to pay tribute to the late Johnny Rogan, whose *Requiem For The Timeless* was a constant source of information. Thanks also to Rob Hughes for his inspiring features in the *Uncut Byrds Ultimate Music Guide* from 2018. Kudos also to *Shindig* magazine for helping keep the spirit of this great music alive while still having the foresight to champion great new music.

Finally, thanks to the musicians who created the music written about in this book. Your restless creativity helped create some of my favourite music.

Just as my first draft was being completed, news arrived of the death of David Crosby. His influence on most of The Byrds' best material is incalculable, and the sound of his dreamy harmonies and flowing melodies will live forever. And perhaps he said it best: 'The Byrds, man, that's important stuff!'.

This book is dedicated to Margaret, who was an avid reader. She would've gotten a kick out of her wee boy writing a book. This one's for you, Mum.

Would you like to write for Sonicbond Publishing?

At Sonicbond Publishing we are always on the look-out for authors, particularly for our two main series:

On Track. Mixing fact with in depth analysis, the On Track series examines the work of a particular musical artist or group. All genres are considered from easy listening and jazz to 60s soul to 90s pop, via rock and metal.

On Screen. This series looks at the world of film and television. Subjects considered include directors, actors and writers, as well as entire television and film series. As with the On Track series, we balance fact with analysis.

While professional writing experience would, of course, be an advantage the most important qualification is to have real enthusiasm and knowledge of your subject. First-time authors are welcomed, but the ability to write well in English is essential.

Sonicbond Publishing has distribution throughout Europe and North America, and all books are also published in E-book form. Authors will be paid a royalty based on sales of their book.

Further details are available from www.sonicbondpublishing.co.uk. To contact us, complete the contact form there or
email info@sonicbondpublishing.co.uk

Foreword

It's my dad's fault, and my sister's. My dad regularly played classical music and jazz in the house when I was growing up. In 1979, Susan bought my first album: *A Tonic for The Troops* by The Boomtown Rats. I've been listening to, reading about and collecting music ever since.

I was first affected by The Byrds in the early 1980s, when it was difficult to find all their albums. There was no Spotify, YouTube, Discogs etc. The 1990s reissue craze hadn't started. On a trip to London in 1983, my dad and I visited Oxford Street. The only Byrds albums you could find in Scotland were mid-price reissues of *Mr. Tambourine Man* or *Fifth Dimension*, and some compilations. But while raking through London's flagship HMV store, there in all its glory was *Younger Than Yesterday*. I stared at the cover for about ten minutes. I had found another of my holy grails.

My initial Byrds obsession was their trilogy of albums recorded in 1966 and 1967. I discovered them in 1982 and was instantly hooked by their otherworldly sound, which was probably a reaction to a lot of contemporary synthesizer and A.O.R. music that my 15-year-old tastes didn't like. And they've been a lifelong love that a few years back saw me write a master's essay called 'Always Beyond Today: How The Byrds' repertoire and musical sources pioneered folk rock, acid rock and country rock sub-genres, and influenced popular music thereafter'. I don't really like these labels. But for the purposes of describing their pioneering work, let's go with them.

When I started writing this book in spring 2022, I was listening to a Soho Radio broadcast by the wonderful *Shindig* magazine. They played a track by The Hanging Stars, and I could hear Byrdsian harmonies and guitars. In 2022. That's the thing: The Byrds' shadow has never gone away. Why is their lineage over 50 years in wingspan? Hopefully, this book will help explain why.

The Byrds' thing was beautiful, and its influence, lasting. They were the original electric music for the mind and body. Their prime happened in the 1960s, which seem like a golden age to us these days. As such, to put The Byrds' work in context, I will speak briefly about the 1960s in the introduction, before considering all their recordings. My knowledge of musical structure is too limited for overly-technical discussion, so the track descriptions don't include much discussion of chord changes or scales. The descriptions are of what I hear, with some back-story context and analysis as to what influenced the writing and recording processes. Also, I refer to us Byrds fans as Byrdmaniacs quite a lot! A few track discussions have significantly more narrative – these cover key recordings that were paradigm-shifting. The reduction in narrative for later albums isn't me flagging near the end, it's just that their later material was generally less interesting. Generally, I've tried to stay objective and not make the first six albums too much of a hagiography. Ultimately, I hope I've put enough life into the tracks – both good and bad – to make you want to listen and form your own opinion. And if it's different from mine, that's fine.

Now for a plea: Chris Hillman thinks Tom Petty was the one person that could've gotten the remaining original Byrds back together. But with Petty's death in 2017, and Croz's recent passing, that chance is gone. However, a proper Byrds documentary similar to 2013's *The Byrd Who Flew Alone* documentary about Gene Clark – but centring on the three musical genres The Byrds pioneered – is still to be made.

Anyway, please enjoy the book, but remember – these are my views. Yours may be different, as it should be. Enjoy your trip Byrdmaniacs, where things may get stranger than known, and where you'll come back younger than now, and always beyond today!

on track ...
The Byrds

Contents

The 1960s: Do You Believe in Magic?

It's difficult to write about the impact of 1960s music succinctly, but it's important to put The Byrds' musical experiments in context. Their pioneering work was recorded during perhaps the most creative musical decade in the history of pop music – or, to be precise, half-decade. While the front cover of *The Freewheelin' Bob Dylan* announced a new pop-culture cool in May 1963, the 1960s really took off in July 1964 when The Beatles' *A Hard Days Night* effectively invented modern pop music.

By the early 1960s, most rock-'n'-roll pioneers were entering bland mediocrity or even obscurity. Using the charts as a barometer, it was one of the worst eras in popular music, where safe *white-bread* acts like Frank Ifield and Pat Boone littered the pop charts with banal pop music. That makes what came just after even more remarkable, because the fertile body of work produced between 1964 and 1969 (justifying the labels of being the most revolutionary and competitive period in pop history) includes some of the most timeless and important music ever recorded. The musical revolutionaries included Bob Dylan – the Woody Guthrie-obsessed folky who was to take literate music into the mainstream – and Brian Wilson, influenced heavily by maverick genius Phil Spector, who scaled new heights of pop composition and arranging. While being anointed the Godfather of Soul, bandleader James Brown invented funk music; Aretha Franklin – after a rather inauspicious start at Columbia – signed to Atlantic Records, becoming the greatest singer of her generation, defining the very essence of soul music; British R&B band The Rolling Stones – specifically from 1968 to 1972 – morphed and justifiably earned the tag of 'greatest rock-'n'-roll band in the world', and former Little Richard backing musician Jimi Hendrix electrified the blues, and invented the rock-guitar hero. There was also Motown – the Detroit 'Motor City' record label that rose from humble beginnings to produce an unparalleled body of work, and made three-minute pop singles fashionable. There were also creative hubs in London, San Francisco, Memphis, New York and countless other fulcrums.

Then there was Liverpool, where the 1960s were conceived on 6 July 1957 at a church fete in Woolton. Mutual friend Ivan Vaughan introduced John Lennon to Paul McCartney, and nothing was ever to be the same again. The Beatles changed everything. They influenced generations of musicians by innovating with everything they did, and at times transformed pop music into art.

In Los Angeles, The Byrds listened to it all. In various incarnations, they investigated unexplored pop music tracts, creating a gumbo of sounds that were to influence their contemporaries, and pioneered musical paths, leaving a musical legacy that's still felt today. They burst onto the scene in that giddy summer of 1965, where instead of giving people what they want, pop musicians began to consider their performances as self-expression. You couldn't turn on the radio without hearing a classic – 'Like a Rolling Stone', '(I Can't Get No) Satisfaction', 'Papa's Got a Brand New Bag', 'My Generation',

'Ticket to Ride', 'Respect', 'Do You Believe in Magic', 'You've Lost That Lovin' Feeling', 'Mr. Tambourine Man' and countless others.

In the 2001 *Walk On By* documentary, British musician Elvis Costello observed, 'It was only in the 1970s that you realised what we lived through in the 1960s. Motown's springiness, the Bacharach melodies and the modernist sound of The Byrds were all happening simultaneously'. In a recent *Rock's Back Pages* podcast, writer Richard Goldstein referred to this era as being like a second jazz age.

Largely forgotten about in the late-1970s, in the early-1980s, a new generation of music fans embraced mid-to-late 1960s pop culture, and The Byrds' guitar stylings and harmonies began to permeate parts of the musical zeitgeist. The 1980s alternative, college and indie music scenes all paid homage to The Byrds and The Velvet Underground, continuing through the 1990s and 2000s. This will be discussed briefly in the legacy chapter at the end of this book.

The Byrds: Always Beyond Today

If you could listen to only one artist all week, who would it be? That was a question posed by David Hepworth in a recent *Word in Your Ear* podcast. Surely it would be the 'Fabs' – moptop era one day, psychedelic the next, post-*Pepper* the following day. It's a bit obvious, though. Or The Rolling Stones – Brian era one day, then Mick Taylor next, then the Ronnie Wood era. What about Bob? – Protest Bob, Thin Wild Mercury Bob, mid-1970s Bob. Surely Joni would work – the earlier songs followed by the jazz-influenced material. But *Blue* is maybe so honest a listen that it would feel like a therapy session.

What about The Byrds? With all they've invented and influenced, their transformative powers took electric guitars to traditional folk music, brought jazz into psychedelic pop and helped the counterculture slowly embrace Nashville. One day folk rock, one-day acid rock, one-day country rock. And you'd still have days left for raga rock, space rock, abstract electronics, early Americana and all the crossover material that defines most of their albums. A week of listening to The Byrds? Their first six studio albums – recorded in three cosmic years – were like a thesis on how to pioneer modern American music.

The Byrds were ahead of their time, always beyond today. They influenced so many of the musical movements that followed as they constantly progressed. Hungry to push the boundaries of popular music, their range and originality created music so inventive that they needed new genres. Their groundbreaking sound, textures and innovations yielded songs that pushed toward the future and opened doors for other musicians. Between 1965 and 1968, they pioneered folk rock, psychedelia and country rock. In essence, they changed the sound of rock 'n' roll, and theirs is the story of helping turn pop into rock.

It's impossible to consider the modern musical landscape without The Byrds, as there have been so many imitators. They even have their own adjective – Byrdsian – describing that chiming 12-string Rickenbacker guitar sound, especially when accompanied by glowing three-part harmonies. Though they were initially known for their radical electrified cover versions, they were also one of the first bands to write their own songs and influence other artists to do the same. Having virtually invented folk rock through their worldwide 1965 hit 'Mr. Tambourine Man', they went on to explore acid rock with their jazz and Eastern-influenced 1966 single 'Eight Miles High', then initiated country rock with the release of *Sweetheart of the Rodeo* in 1968. By investigating their repertoire and exploring their work, I'll consider what influenced the group's tastes and innovations in popular music, and contemplate their legacy.

The roots of the band go back to a rather preppy commercial folk scene full of folk purists who hated rock 'n' roll, and by the early-1960s, guitarist Jim McGuinn wanted to get into something else. The fact that no original members came from a rock background was crucial to the creation of their sound, which had roots also in country, bluegrass, blues and even jazz. Initially, they were folkies who became Beatle-ised Dylans. The Byrds might easily have evolved without Dylan, but never without The Beatles. By 1964, McGuinn didn't want to combine folk and rock as much as just imitate what The Beatles were doing, with passing folk chords. Gene Clark and David Crosby were also astounded by The Beatles' audacity, and the pair left the staid folk world behind after they saw the movie *A Hard Days Night*. Soon The Byrds would help put the death knell in the folk scene, via the new British-invasion sound.

It's not that someone wouldn't have stumbled into playing folk songs on an electric guitar – indeed, The Searchers and The Beau Brummels predated The Byrds in anticipating the folk rock sound with their chiming guitars and soaring harmonies. However, it was defined by The Byrds' musical authority – especially that of Jim Roger McGuinn, whose eclectic taste and 12-string expertise were beyond most pop interpreters of the time. More than any other act, The Byrds were responsible for conceiving folk rock, by combining The Beatles' backbeat with lyrical components of folk music. Dylan and The Beatles were the catalysts for folk rock, but The Byrds delivered it through those harmonies and arrangements, and provided the basis for much of the new pop of the next two years.

After their folk rock beginnings, they plunged into a psychedelic whirlwind with a new repertoire that included the transformative 'Eight Miles High', inspired by John Coltrane's tenor-sax solos. As the cultural significance shifted in the late-1960s from the single to the album, each new window of The Byrds' psychedelic world produced essential music, including sub-genres like space rock, raga rock, and a stony pastoral rock mainly via their stupendous Holy Trinity of albums: *Fifth Dimension, Younger Than Yesterday* and *The Notorious Byrd Brothers*. They also pioneered country rock with the release of *Sweetheart of the Rodeo*. In just two years, these psychedelic pilots had become acid hillbillies. Though not initially popular with rock or country audiences, the album has had a lasting impact on everyone from 1970s singer-songwriters to the 1990s alternative country movement.

At the end of 1968, The Byrds became a backing band and a front for Roger McGuinn, and opinion is divided about the quality of post-*Sweetheart* albums. But it's fair to say that none of them had the same innovative quality of the group's classic 1965-1968 period. Later Byrds material tended to suffer from the law of diminishing returns. After six more studio albums – from two decent 1969 albums, through their creative nadir of the early-1970s to the poorly-received 1973 reunion album – they split up.

The group's time in the commercial sun only lasted for around a year, but today they are revered as one of the most innovative and influential acts of their era. They yielded three different sounds that have remained part of rock culture. As well as influencing their peers such as The Beatles and Bob Dylan, The Byrds' innovation has reverberated through the work of The Eagles, The Pretenders, The Smiths, R.E.M., and current acts like Fleet Foxes and The Sadies, featuring those jangling guitars, drony psychedelia, twangy country guitars, and of course, those harmonies.

Meet The Byrds

From 1965 to 1968, everything from Bach and Coltrane to bluegrass and early synthesizers blended into The Byrds' folky mix. But to help understand those innovations, it's important to look at the original members' backgrounds. All were folk or bluegrass musicians, who met in the Los Angeles folk scene. Jim McGuinn (born 13 July 1942, Chicago) was already a studio veteran who was part of the New York Brill Building team, clocking in and out to write pop songs in the early-1960s. (His name is still legally Jim. He changed his middle name from Joseph to Roger in 1967, and uses Roger as a stage name.) Encouraged by Bobby Darin, McGuinn moved West to pursue a solo career. Though he was a folk musician, he wanted to get into something less stale, as he felt the folk scene was becoming low-quality, and by 1964 he'd also become obsessed with the music of The Beatles. He performed folk with a backbeat, but no one liked it much – except for one guy who went backstage to meet him. His name was Harold Eugene Clark (born 17 November 1944, Missouri).

They'd both served apprenticeships as sidemen with a variety of folk artists and seasoned entertainers. While McGuinn had worked with The Limeliters and Chad Mitchell Trio, Clark had played with The New Christy Minstrels. Clark was also starting to write Beatlesque songs, and the pair became a duo.

Soon they had a *stalker* fan in another singer. David Crosby (born 14 August 1941, Los Angeles) had been working with Les Baxter's Balladeers. His father had been Oscar-nominated for his cinematography on the 1952 western movie *High Noon*. Crosby introduced himself to Clark (he already knew McGuinn) at the Troubadour club by muscling-in to fill out the top notes of their harmonies. Initially reticent to become a trio, McGuinn and Clark mostly sang in unison, but they agreed that Crosby seemed to have a sixth sense as to where to drop in a second harmony. With Crosby's higher vocal range, they could go further than most bands, as he had more room to develop his harmonies. The duo became a trio. Before The Byrds, harmony singing in rock 'n' roll meant doo-wop, the Everly Brothers countrified harmonies, or the sound of groups like The Four Freshmen that would later be developed by The Beach Boys. But The Byrds' harmonies were something else altogether: simultaneously traditional and modern.

Folk music was at the heart of everything they sang, and those soon-to-be-imitated harmonies made their live debut at The Troubadour Club in Los Angeles in 1964. Initially called The Jet Set, Crosby introduced McGuinn and Clark to Jim Dickson, who could see the trio's potential. With his recording industry contacts, Dickson became their manager. He managed to arrange rehearsal time at World Pacific Studios, and the band started to develop their sound – a combination of their own Beatles-influenced material and traditional folk. They recorded a flop single under the awful British-sounding name The Beefeaters: 'Please Let Me Love You', issued on Elektra in October 1964. But they didn't sign to the label, as boss Jac Holzman thought they wanted too much money.

By now, Crosby was a reluctant bass player, so Dickson suggested bluegrass and mandolin player Chris Hillman (born 4 April 1944, Los Angeles) as The Jet Set's bassist. Hillman's background included stints with bluegrass groups The Scottsville Squirrel Barkers and The Hillmen. Hillman later joked that when he went to the first recording session, he thought The Jet Set were a skiffle group, due to their primitive instruments and setup.

With Crosby moving to rhythm guitar, all they needed was a drummer. Dickson suggested prototype slacker Michael Clarke (born 3 June 1946, Washington), mainly because he looked like a taller Brian Jones, and Clarke joined, completing the jigsaw. He was a local conga player when Dickson asked him to join, but contrary to popular myth, he *had* played drums before.

Having great vision, Dickson's influence on the group cannot be underestimated. Even in the band's early days, he could foresee the possible effect of McGuinn's artistic restlessness, Clark's songwriting potential, Hillman's bluegrass influence and Crosby's love of jazz harmony and song structures. Dickson also knew Miles Davis, who recommended Columbia Records sign the band. (Legend also has it that Lenny Bruce's mother got them their first paying gig: at East Los Angeles College.) On 10 November 1964, they accepted Columbia Records contract offer, and set about recording some traditional folk songs and a few band originals (mainly by Gene Clark). Influenced by McGuinn's fascination with flight, they aped the then-current moniker-misspelling craze, and changed their name to The Byrds.

The strongest catalyst for their folk rock sound goes back to The Beatles' 1964 film *A Hard Days Night*. Also attracted to the songs and screaming fans, The Byrds were affected by George Harrison's Rickenbacker guitar sound. McGuinn was especially attracted to the jangling arpeggiated fade on the title track. They were fascinated by how The Beatles married a rock-'n'-roll backbeat to folk changes and harmonies, helping synthesize a new type of music. Ultimately it was the creativity of The Beatles which swung McGuinn, Clark and Crosby away from folk, and took Hillman from bluegrass. Also influenced by the sparkling guitar sound of The Searchers – especially 'Needles and Pins' and 'When You Walk in the Room' – The Byrds were now a fully-formed electric band at the embryonic stage of merging these disparate streams to create something new.

In late-1964 – under Dickson's guidance – they recorded demos that were eventually released as *Preflyte* in 1969. These demos will be discussed in the 'Connected Flights' part of the *Mr. Tambourine Man* chapter. The bare demos now sound a little rough and dated, and since The Byrds all started out as Beatles imitators, the British group's influence is obvious. However, the recordings now stand as a historical document in the gestation of transformative music. Upon the release of *Preflyte*, *Rolling Stone* magazine commented on how the sessions recalled the birth of a band that had contributed more to rock than anyone else on their side of the Atlantic.

The Byrds were taking flight, and their merging of folk and rock with trademark harmonies was beginning to surface. Though this was a hybrid Beatles sound, it was also undeniably an American sound of sunny Californian cool. Gene Clark was already displaying a skill for emotive lyrics, and an ear for minor-chord pop melancholy, and the group were also becoming versed in covering other writers' songs. One writer, in particular, was becoming a major source of material.

Interlude: Jingle Jangle Mornings

Jack Holzman later regretted not giving the band the money they wanted when they recorded the Beefeaters single. But Jim Dickson eventually secured the $5000 investment from another source – Naomi Hirshhorn: a client of the group's co-manager Eddie Tickner. They needed drums for Clarke and a new bass for Hillman. It also meant that McGuinn could buy his Rickenbacker electric 12-string!

Meanwhile, Jim Dickson had obtained a demo of an unreleased Bob Dylan song called 'Mr. Tambourine Man', which he felt would make a great electric single version. But the band were initially unimpressed. The incongruous military marching-band drum pattern and stiff vocals of early demos were at odds with the song's melody and surreal lyricism. Their demos sounded thin – enter McGuinn's new Rickenbacker.

The group now set about recording their debut single, and unwittingly – through McGuinn's flair for experimentation, Clark's blossoming songwriting and Crosby crafting the vocal harmonies – were about to transform popular music.

Mr. Tambourine Man (1965)

Personnel:
Jim McGuinn: 12 string guitar, vocals
Gene Clark: tambourine, vocals
David Crosby: rhythm guitar, vocals
Chris Hillman: bass, vocals
Michael Clarke: drums
Producer: Terry Melcher
Record label: Columbia, CBS (UK)
Release date: 21 June 1965
Chart position: UK: 7, US 6
Running time: 31:35

By early 1965, much of The Byrds' in-concert repertoire was Dylan material. At this stage he was recording his *Bringing It All Back Home* album, which had a side each of acoustic and electric songs. The group envisaged taking this a stage further by combining Dylan's literate folk songs with a Beatles backbeat. McGuinn particularly steered the The Byrds towards rock-'n'-roll-inspired folk music, where he saw Dylan and The Beatles as the driving forces of the time.

Dickson was still keen to champion 'Mr. Tambourine Man', and McGuinn now saw the potential in the intelligent lyric content wed to electric guitar riffs and a solid backbeat. In January 1965, The Byrds entered Columbia Studios to record the song as their debut single. Columbia was then a rather square label, though credit should go to the label's hip executive Billy James who became a cheerleader for The Byrds' hit-making potential. (He would also write the debut album liner notes.)

Since the band had only been together for a few months, the other Columbia executives backed producer Terry Melcher's decision to go with the L.A. session unit known as The Wrecking Crew as backing musicians, and only McGuinn played on 'Mr. Tambourine Man' and its B-side 'I Knew I'd Want You'. By the time the album sessions began in March, the band *was* deemed professional enough to record it, though the use of session musicians on the debut single has often prompted the misconception that the band didn't play on their debut album.

By this time, the band's residency at Ciro's nightclub had already made them a must-see L.A. act, and teenagers filled the club, desperate to see the *local Beatles* perform. McGuinn's vocals and phrasing were now pitched somewhere between Dylan and Lennon. They were playing five sets a night, and because McGuinn didn't have time to stop playing and change from finger-pick to plectrum, he played two styles at once: flat-picking and finger-picking. McGuinn learned this from his banjo playing days and this would influence the jingle jangle arpeggios that would underpin The Byrds' sound.

The group's decision to re-record 'Mr. Tambourine Man' was epochal: six months later, it became the first transatlantic folk rock hit, and the band's harmonies and McGuinn's Rickenbacker sound would soon be much imitated. The album's tracks merged Beatle-ised interpretations of Bob Dylan and Pete Seeger songs with strong, pop-based originals. In addition to four Dylan covers, it also saw the emergence of Gene Clark as a major songwriter. The new sound was the opening blast in the folk rock boom.

Following the transatlantic number-1 success of the single, the band were quickly labelled as America's Beatles, while Britain's *NME* referred to a new phenomenon: Byrdmania! The *NME* also predicted the band would become one of the biggest American groups ever. Even George Harrison called them America's Beatles. No pressure!

The Byrds exerted an enormous influence on their contemporaries, and no other US band did more to stop the tide of British Invasion bands conquering the States, as the album represented the first effective American challenge. Though others had dabbled with electric instruments, The Byrds seemed to clarify the whole situation, and their authoritative music was seen as the antithesis to the overly-manufactured Brill Building music that had been dominating the US pop charts before the British Invasion. Musicians from folk and rock soon turned to Rickenbacker guitars to electrify traditional material, and included two and three-part vocal harmonies. In L.A., this included Buffalo Springfield – with the youthful Stephen Stills and Neil Young – and Love, where Byrds roadie Bryan McLean would join up with local songwriter Arthur Lee. Their debut album was full of Byrdsian nods, and Love guitarist Johnny Echols admitted that everybody in Hollywood was influenced by The Byrds. The hit single had opened up a new audience for the band and their contemporaries – generally, by late 1965, session musicians got more work if they could replicate the new folk rock sound. The Byrds had raised the stakes for other L.A. bands like The Turtles and The Leaves, who looked to them as the catalyst for their own music.

San Francisco bands like Jefferson Airplane were also influenced by The Byrds. Their folky leader Marty Balin had visited L.A., and the *Mr. Tambourine Man* album had sent him beetling back to San Francisco to form a folk rock band. Seasoned folk musician John Philips saw the potential too, and immediately disbanded his group The Journeymen (who'd stopped performing a rather stale version of 'Mr. Tambourine Man'), as he felt there was no point anymore. Instead, his new folk rock harmony group, The Mamas & the Papas, came back from the Virgin Islands and used the folk rock template to restructure 'California Dreamin'' and start their run of hits. On the East Coast, The Lovin' Spoonful used their jug band leanings to create a more cute brand of folk rock. Not everything has stood the test of time, though, and in retrospect, some folk rock material now sounds too cute or even clumsy: like Barry McGuire's raspy version of P.F. Sloan's 'Eve of Destruction'.

Record companies also saw the commercial appeal of folk rock – perhaps the best example of manufacturing an acoustic song and fashioning it for the electric world being when Columbia hired session musicians to overdub 12-string, bass and drums on Paul Simon's 'The Sound of Silence'. Previously an acoustic track, the song joined the folk rock bandwagon and became a US number one at the start of 1966. The irony of it being recast with a Byrds sound wasn't lost on Simon, who claimed McGuinn played acoustic guitar on the song's original demo.

The Byrds musical soundscapes also created a transatlantic communication. The Beatles reciprocated by using The Byrds' dreamy atmosphere for 'Nowhere Man'. The Byrds were now representatives of a whole subculture, and were the catalyst in bringing the Sunset Strip scene to Ciro's, and influenced the first incarnation of flower children. They were the must-see band on the Sunset strip and played Jane Fonda's 4th of July party, mingling with the Fondas, Jack Nicholson, Mia Farrow and Warren Beatty.

The album's front cover featured a Barry Feinstein fisheye lens band photo, oozing aloof California cool while looking a bit like *Carnaby St Yanks*, before the green suede capes and granny glasses took over later in the year. The back cover included a photo of Bob Dylan performing with the group. Cool artwork would be a feature of future Byrds albums. Clearly, Columbia – even if they didn't fully understand the music inside – were following Elektra in making art out of the record sleeve. By the end of 1965, the album cover influenced the fisheye cover image of The Beatles' *Rubber Soul*.

Mr. Tambourine Man became not only the sound of the Sunset Strip but the sound of L.A. and, finally the sound of the nation. Before The Byrds, rock 'n' roll on the Sunset Strip consisted of bands covering tired R&B tunes. But the group's music was cerebral, feeding the body and mind – especially with Dylan's songs. Never had lyrics of such literary quality been on a pop record. The music offered poetry with a message and a beat, and was unlike anything in pop at the time.

'Mr. Tambourine Man' (Dylan)

If The Byrds had only recorded this one song, they would still hold a place in rock history. With its classic Rickenbacker sound and surreal lyric coated in a chorus of soaring, heavenly harmonies, it introduced the first of their hypnotic drones.

Written by Bob Dylan in late-1964, the song was inspired by a huge Turkish frame drum used by his guitarist Bruce Langhorne, which Dylan thought looked like a tambourine. He didn't release his first version, since Ramblin' Jack Elliott was out of tune. Byrds manager Jim Dickson didn't think the rock-'n'-roll songs McGuinn and Clark were writing had enough substance, and pressured them to record it. Since the early Byrds were influenced by – but not necessarily imitative of – The Beatles, Dickson suggested The Byrds record an electrified 'Beatley' version, and auditioned them all for the lead singer role, which McGuinn won. Initially, the band were reluctant to release it as they thought it lacked commercial appeal, especially with its five-minute length. But McGuinn was busy rearranging the song with important input from Terry Melcher. They removed three of the four verses, already thinking of ways it could be played on AM radio. They kept the verse mentioning boot heels, as that would be associated with the Beatles' look. Using another Beatles trick, the song started with – and was built around – its exultant chorus. Verse two was placed between the choruses, and though it removes much of the song's ambiguity, it still retains its mystery. With lines like 'Take me on a trip on your magic swirling ship', it was unlike anything else heard on pop radio.

Melcher hired Wrecking Crew musicians Hal Blaine (drums), Larry Knechtel (bass), Leon Russell (electric piano) and Jerry Cole (who perfectly pitched the chink-chink guitar refrain from The Beach Boys 'Don't Worry Baby' for his rhythm guitar part) for the track, along with McGuinn's jangling 12-string Rickenbacker. McGuinn wanted the bass to complement his guitar with countermelodies. On future Byrds recordings, Chris Hillman would become exceptional at this. Meanwhile, McGuinn based the song's intro on Bach's 'Jesu, Joy of Man's Desiring', and audio compression was added. Melcher also suggested the opening bass line, which gave the song an instant hook, and persuaded Hal Blaine to play heavier on the snare drum. McGuinn later gave credit to Melcher for getting the sound so creamy, and felt he had a great ear for pop records.

McGuinn added his vocals only days after being initiated into the Subud faith, and later revealed he was thinking of spiritual concepts, such as taking him away from the bomb, irrespective of what Dylan's lyric actually meant. Over the lead vocal, McGuinn, Crosby and Clark added their crystalline harmonies. The condensed harmonies were perfectly structured, with significant input from Dean Webb of The Dillards, who suggested they record a harmony demo for Dickson to show Crosby exactly what he wanted.

The difference between this version and the World Pacific version is astonishing. The new version was an invitation to a party, especially compared to Dylan's more sarcastic take. McGuinn felt that changing the song from a 2/4 to 4/4 time signature was key, because it rocked. Crosby said he could see the wheels turning in Dylan's brain when he first heard The Byrds electrify his song. He was so impressed with the transformation, and was amazed that you could dance to it, barely recognising his own song. Dylan's comments gave them the biggest indication yet of how much an electric band could transform an acoustic song. Pop music didn't really feel the effect of Dylan's influence until The Byrds hit with 'Mr. Tambourine Man', and by Beatle-ising the song into pre-eminence, it gave Dylan a new vision of his own music.

Dickson was vital in setting the group's sights high in terms of repertoire and told them to aim for something lasting with substance and depth, and not just a quick hit. With this recording, they achieved both. In *The Heart of Rock and Soul*, Dave Marsh memorably summarised that while the vocals are sweet, they didn't need to be up to much, because they were set against the greatest electric 12-string guitar riff ever created.

Though the track was recorded in January 1965, it was shelved until April. Initially, Columbia didn't really know what to do with a rock-'n'-roll act. Indeed, while waiting for the song to be released, Dino Valente suggested that he and McGuinn form a group to wear spacesuits and sing into wireless mics. McGuinn considered it but, thankfully, decided to stick it out with The Byrds.

KRLA liked the single, and L.A Beatlemania DJ, Dave Hull, picked it as his 'Tip for a Hit'. By the end of the week, it took off throughout the West, and the following week was on New York's regional chart. As new fans arrived from San Francisco to see The Byrds at Ciros, the band heard it played twice in a row on the radio, and couldn't believe it. Crosby referred to it as being like a tidal wave washing over them. Before it took off, Dylan's manager Albert Grossman tried to stop its release, but was too late, and Bob was already in the loop anyway.

The opening of this landmark pop single still sends a rush every time I hear it! Folk rock was something completely different, and contributed to the death of the commercial folk scene, as executives realised the new sound sold better, and the single spearheaded the mid-1960s folk rock boom when a number of Byrds-influenced acts had hits. But The Byrds were the first authentic folk/rock fusion, born in 140 seconds. The song was a fanfare for a new rock-'n'-roll sound where 'Mr. Tambourine Man' became one of the songs of summer 1965 – a summer of pop anthems. The Beatles 'Ticket to Ride' with its chiming guitars, set the scene, followed by the vitriol of The Rolling Stones' 'Satisfaction', while the end of summer was heralded by Dylan's 'Like a Rolling Stone'.

'I'll Feel a Whole Lot Better' (Clark)

Several Gene Clark originals were included in The Byrds' early repertoire, including this quintessential Byrdsian track. With its origins of jangle and power pop – and a little country and western, too – this whirling Beatlesy stampede lifted the spirits of teens and serious music fans with its delirious anthemic stomp. The structurally simple song was kept engaging all the way through gripping chord changes and the opening-chorus harmonies building as the song progresses. (Note that the guitars change from single to dual channels at the start too.) The bass line sees Hillman get into his groove, and with the wonderful converging, cosmic choral harmonies and lush guitars, it's a prophetic 12-string symphony for tomorrow. In particular, the guitar break evokes the start of the counterculture – those 30 seconds encapsulate the Ciro's scene perfectly. Terry Melcher was said to be overwhelmed by the quality of this recording, and the track partly belongs to him, with his trebly percussion-based production swimming in echo and phasing.

The song – about a girl who Clark thought was stalking him – is a bridge between his early sentimental ballads and later introspective material. This is perfectly illustrated by his use of cynical romanticism, where he inserts the keyword 'probably', as in 'I'll *probably* feel a whole lot better', and this subtext lends the song a certain Dylan/Lennon ambiguity. Clark later admitted he'd based the melody on the riff from The Searchers' 'Needles and Pins' and wrote the song in about 20 minutes. It's clearly an *early* Byrds song, as their L.A. roots are evident, especially on the alternate take on the CD reissue, though Clark's vocals are too stiff on that version.

The song has become a folk rock standard, with many critics rightly considering it one of the band's and Clark's best. It's ironic that it was a B-side and better than its A-side 'All I Really Want To Do', as some DJs plugged 'I'll Feel a Whole Lot Better' more. A cover of the song by Tom Petty in 1989 produced some much-needed royalties for Gene Clark, but sadly he barely lived long enough to enjoy the new income.

It's a timeless slice of hypnotic, bittersweet pop that most bands would have killed for as an A-side, and the group's agility with different styles was becoming apparent. It remains a fan favourite.

'Spanish Harlem Incident' (Dylan)
'Mr. Tambourine Man' became a valuable asset for Bob Dylan. When The Byrds continued to record his songs, he told McGuinn it gave him a real boost. 'Spanish Harlem Incident' originally appeared on *Another Side of Bob Dylan* in 1964, and the band had played it regularly during their pre-fame sets at Ciros.

This is an acceptable-but-shaky rendition, where McGuinn came up with the guitar part while Hillman developed the bass part, which includes a few fluffed lines. Apparently, Hillman's string broke and made a flap sound on the 'I've been wondering all about me' line, but Melcher kept it in.

Overall, McGuinn's brazen vocal and the short playing time ensure that it's not one of their most inspired Dylan covers. While not wanting to define early Byrds songs as verse/chorus/12-string guitar break etc., this could've done with a McGuinn solo. In hindsight, a *Preflyte* leftover like Clark's 'For Me Again' could've been a better choice as an album track.

'You Won't Have to Cry' (Clark, McGuinn)
This beautiful arrangement survived the World Pacific sessions with divine Rickenbacker picking from McGuinn, and some of the group's most luxurious harmonies. It's a tender and poetic mid-tempo ballad, with the woman now portrayed as the sufferer rather than the predator of 'I'll Feel a Whole Lot Better'.

It was arranged with shifting high harmonies prominent, and had a strong *Beatles for Sale* influence. The Crosby-influenced harmonies – especially in the bridge – are a clear marker for future Crosby, Stills & Nash work, such as those on 'You Don't Have to Cry' and 'Helplessly Hoping' on their debut. In fact, this song's peculiar structure comes off like an offbeat bluegrass song, and is possibly linked to McGuinn originally assuming that The Beatles' passing minor chords all stemmed from bluegrass. The alternate take on the CD reissue is similar, albeit slightly slower, and some Crosby harmonies more audible, which is rarely a bad thing. Both are much better than the *Preftyte* version, which has a rather clumsy, blustery drum rhythm, but this album version is best, where Clark and McGuinn sound as one.

If The Byrds had recorded this for their second album, they might've had the confidence to include a Rickenbacker solo. It would've also been nice to hear them perform this during the Clarence White years, with one of his economical bluegrass breaks included.

'Here Without You' (Clark)

This combines major and minor keys, and has an eerie, gothic atmosphere, with folk rather than rock-'n'-roll changes. Crosby always loved the chord structure and infectious haunting melody, and felt that Clark always had a skill with melody over minor chords.

Clark positively croons, like a folk-rock pop idol. He also foresees melancholy indie pop with the Morrissey-like lyric 'Streets that I walk on depress me'. The lyric describes a trip through streets, which intensifies his pining for an absent lover, like a hymn to beautiful hurt. The pending tension suggests a more reflective sensitivity – the sort of vulnerability Lennon was starting to convey in his songs. The 'I'll see you someday' ending suggests the separation is short-term. This is one of Clark's most introspective lost love songs. On the debut, he sang his songs with a nervous tension that was relieved by Crosby's harmony – he always knew how to inhabit a Clark song – and those glorious stretched melancholy harmonies are reminiscent of The Searchers.

A raw version appeared on *Preflyte*, and the song has been covered many times, with a particularly moving version by Richard Thompson, Clive Gregson and Christine Collister on the late-1980s *Time Between* Byrds tribute album.

'The Bells of Rhymney' (Davies, Seeger)

McGuinn had already arranged a version of this for Judy Collins a year earlier, and The Byrds' version was another example of them standing at the crossroads of folk and pop, with layers of 12-strings and ghostly medieval harmonies. They also worked on this one while high on LSD!

It tracks the basic melodic shifts of Pete Seeger's earlier version which was based on his adaptation of 'Twinkle Twinkle Little Star'. But McGuinn's languid 12-string, Clarke's cool, laid-back drumming and the extraordinary gliding harmonies at the end place The Byrds in an entirely idiosyncratic tangent. In revamping the song, McGuinn changed 'Who robbed the miner' to 'Who killed the miner', and added passing chords, creating a more-edgy interpretation.

You can hear another Bach influence on the guitar solo halfway through, which includes gorgeous banjo-like picking. The track incorporates blaring guitar chords, a humming bass and a bombastic rock-bottom drum rhythm, all appropriate for dancing. Jim Dickson reckoned that Michael Clarke's cymbals were the most important thing on the record, as it became a dance-floor sensation at Ciro's nightclub. In fact, he felt Clarke's cymbals were too quiet in Melcher's mono mix, so in the stereo mix, they were considerably raised in level.

Though Dickson maintained that the studio version never reached the heights of the band's live renditions at Ciro's, this version was monumentally important in the progression of their sound. This is where psych folk begins. In the closing verse, wordless vocals melt towards the heavens. In his *Psychedelia* book, Rob Chapman reckons the wordless, blissed-out coda became one of the key motifs of psychedelia. The Byrds invented it on this track.

George Harrison admitted that he included this track's main guitar figure in The Beatles' 'If I Needed Someone' on *Rubber Soul*. John Lennon was listening too – he described the 'Norwegian Wood' melody as his attempt to forge Oriental intervals introduced to him by The Byrds.

This track was extraordinary. Their echoey treatment of the gloomy subject matter gave the song a euphoric Pacific-breeze lift. Hippies were now dancing to this: a song about a Welsh mining disaster and oppressed miners!

'All I Really Want to Do' (Dylan)
An alternative take of this became the next single. While the album version is slightly more pedestrian, the mono single used the 'I don't want to' opening instead of 'I ain't looking', and is the better take. It's amazing that anyone was inventive enough to transform the song and see a possible hit in it, especially given Dylan's awkward version on *Another Side of Bob Dylan* the year before.

The song had already gone down well in concert, where The Byrds' version of Dylan's slightly dreary song became euphoric. McGuinn added Beatles' chords to produce a sublime chorus. This version also has a different structure, where they made the bridge sound more Beatles-like.

The band were worried about releasing another Dylan song as a single, not wanting to be formulaic. But the record company believed another Dylan cover would produce another hit. Columbia was also keen to win a chart war since Cher had also released the song as a single, so Columbia rush-released The Byrds' take while 'Mr. Tambourine Man' was still in the charts, hoping it would stall the success of Cher's version. However, Cher's inferior take – a diluted version of The Byrds' interpretation – was the bigger hit in the USA. The Byrds' version only reached number 40, though it *did* reach the UK top 5. In their single review, the *New Musical Express* assumed it would be another number one.

McGuinn later commented that what bugged him most was Dylan telling him he was upset Cher had 'beaten' them in the charts, and McGuinn felt Dylan had lost some faith in him.

'I Knew I'd Want You' (Clark)
Compared to the ploddier version from the World Pacific sessions, this song was reborn as a chiming, brooding ballad in 6/8 time. With its 'Oh Yeah' refrain and hip turn of phrase 'You've had me on your trip', it still sounds like a benchmark for early indie rock.

The track was cut with the Wrecking Crew, and this version was recorded at the same session as 'Mr. Tambourine Man', and became its B-side. That means it's Larry Knechtel on bass, and not Chris Hillman.

The Byrds certainly sounded like a new band compared to their earlier recordings, and though the *Preflyte* version is perfectly decent (except for its slightly lumbering rhythm), their arranging confidence was increasing. Byrds' biographer Johnny Rogan reckoned this minor-key Beatlesque shuffle would've launched The Byrds' career had they not had the Dylan songs. But as glorious as this song is, 'I'll Feel a Whole Lot Better' or 'The Bells of Rhymney' would probably both have launched the band more successfully.

'It's No Use' (Clark, McGuinn)
One of two McGuinn/Clark co-writes on the album, this dates from the previous year, when they started writing songs together. It's a rock-'n'-roll song tentatively entering the folk world with its opening Chuck Berry riff, but the band stay true to their folk roots with their melancholy harmonies. There are early hints of psychedelia from McGuinn with his spidery Rickenbacker guitar break, and in that sense, it's another classic Byrds' transitional track, bordering two ages of rock. Despite the harmonies, it's certainly less folky than the other material here.

The vocals here are the fruition of a number of takes. (An earlier take appeared on the Sundazed 2001 *Preflyte* reissue). McGuinn and Clark now sang the melody, and Crosby sang the only harmony, which he originally found difficult due to the chord structure. There's also an alternate take on the CD reissue, with a more-laboured lead guitar break from McGuinn, and a more-punchy ending.

While this track has good intentions – particularly in trying to break free from the folk idiom – for all its psyche guitar feel, the song doesn't quite go anywhere. In retrospect, McGuinn's guitar break gently pre-empted what would come later. The song is also proof of why Dickson thought they needed more outside material.

'Don't Doubt Yourself Babe' (DeShannon)
With maraca and tambourine, this sounded not unlike The Rolling Stones' version of 'Not Fade Away'. 'Don't Doubt Yourself Babe' made the final track list as a thank you to Jackie DeShannon, who championed the band in their early *preflyte* days. (They appeared as the backing band on her 'Splendour in the Grass' track.)

This was a decent – if not hugely successful – move away from their more-jangly guitar work – McGuinn including a Bo Diddley rhythm and trance-inducing echo. Though there's a lovely echoey guitar fade-out at the end, it could've done with more work – especially the half-baked instrumental break. But as usual, the harmonies are bright: especially the 'ooooh's at the end of each verse. Sounding like a work in progress, the intro's embryonic guitar part sounds like an attempt at the intro that eventually graced the next track.

'Chimes of Freedom' (Dylan)

McGuinn's vocals have rarely been better than on this – one of the band's most-loved cover versions. It was recorded on the album's final recording day – a date that foresaw future Byrds friction when manager Dickson had to stop a fight instigated by Crosby. He was still hopeful of getting 'Hey Joe' on the record (more of that in 1966), and acted up during the recording. After the obstinate Byrd referred to the song as a 'dumb cowboy song', Dickson eventually throttled him and sat on his chest until he completed his vocal part. It proved to be one of those great exorcising moments, as Crosby got his frustration out his system and never sang it better, contributing a beautiful backing vocal to McGuinn's fractured lead. Everyone loved it, including the stubborn Crosby, who was so pleased with it that he was moved to tears.

It's another track where Dylan's poetry is heightened by the dazzling invention of McGuinn's cascading guitar notes. Tantalisingly, they considered releasing a mono single of this with 'The Bells of Rhymney' on the flip. What a perfect portrayal of 1965 Byrds that would've been, especially since Terry Melcher had remixed the track to make it sound more like their performances at Ciros. Thankfully, these versions can be found on the Sundazed 2004 *Cancelled Flytes* singles box set.

Dylan first performed the song at the 1964 Newport Folk Festival before it was even released on *Another Side of Bob Dylan* a few months later. The Byrds kept the song in their live repertoire well into the 1970s, and a good live version appears on *Live At The Fillmore 1969* (released in 2000), featuring Clarence White on guitar. Most cover versions use The Byrds' church-bell folk-rock template as opposed to Dylan's straight acoustic version, such as the 1970s version by Byrds fanatics Starry Eyed and Laughing.

As well as influencing Bob Dylan himself – whose collaborator Mike Bloomfield confirmed that Dylan now wanted The Byrds' sound included in his repertoire – The Byrds were now influencing the emerging counterculture, where their version of 'Chimes of Freedom' became a ringing hippie protest call.

'We'll Meet Again' (Parker, Charles)

This World War II anthem came into their live set at Ciro's. They knew it from the end of Stanley Kubrick's *Dr Strangelove* movie, where it was played over the end credits. So in an emerging counterculture sense, it was the perfect homage to finish the album with. As such, The Byrds' polite version was laced with irony, and in 1965 this was probably an amusing and audacious album ending. This was still an era when albums tended to include tedious filler, so a satirical track like this was unusual, and it was the first of their trademark *quirky* album endings. The eerie burst of distorted guitar at the end gives the track a certain portentous feel – a sound that would become part of the fabric of the emerging rock music.

These days it's more difficult to get excited about the track (except for McGuinn's solo), and it now seems like a bit of a throwaway – especially when the joke of the satirically-polite vocals is now nearly 60 years old. But in the context of 1965, it was quite daring in concept, if not execution.

Connected Flights
'She Has a Way' (Clark)
This should've been included on the album, but was left off at the 11th hour for sounding too much like The Beatles, and to make way for outside material: a decision that would also blight later Byrds albums.

Written in 1964, it still sounds like a gorgeous prototype of jangly sunshine pop, where Clark doesn't sound so forlorn – the song being more optimistic than some of his later melancholy songs. The version on *Preflyte* – clearly influenced by The Everly Brothers' tight harmonies – is superior to that on the 1988 *In The Beginning* compilation. This also appears on the CD reissue and the *Cancelled Flights* box set, as it was earmarked for the B-side of the unreleased 'The Times They Are a-Changin'' single.

It's not straight-ahead folk rock like the other tracks, but it would've sat better on the album than did their average rendition of 'Spanish Harlem Incident'. And in retrospect, it could've replaced 'We'll Meet Again', and 'Chimes of Freedom' could've instead been a clarion-call album ending.

'You and Me' (McGuinn, Clark, Crosby)
No writer details exist for this backing track, so when released on the mid-1990s CD album reissue, it was assumed the three of them wrote it. The song had been a live favourite prior to 'Mr. Tambourine Man' becoming a hit, but was dropped in favour of newer Gene Clark songs. It's a tantalising Byrds-by-numbers track – a great one for Byrds fanatics, but not essential. In truth, it plods along until the punchy ending.

Beefeaters Single
'Please Let Me Love You' (Clark, McGuinn, Gerst)
With their British-sounding moniker, this sounded like a Beatles knockoff, especially the McCartney-style phrasing. It was sung by McGuinn, Clark and Crosby, but session musicians played the backing. The Gene Clark bridge is the best thing in the song. By the time they changed their name to The Byrds, they never bothered with it.

27

'Don't Be Long' (McGuinn, Gerst)

Featuring the same session musicians as above, this was renamed 'It Won't Be Wrong' when recorded for The Byrds' second album. But the version here is a rigid, perfunctory run-through, and shows little of the band's potential.

Preflyte songs not included on *Mr. Tambourine Man*

In July 1969, Gary Usher's Together label released demo recordings from the group's 1964 rehearsals at World Pacific Studios as the *Preflyte* album. It's notable as possibly the earliest example of a collection of outtakes by a major rock artist. These tracks either appeared on *Preflyte* or the *Preflyte Plus* reissue. Some alternative mixes also appeared on Rhino's *In The Beginning* compilation.

'You Showed Me' (McGuinn, Clark)

This was a future hit for The Turtles (who slowed it right down), and was subsequently covered by The Lightning Seeds and Salt-N-Pepa, and sampled by U2.

   The *Preflyte* version is a bare semi-acoustic version and is early proof of Clark's imminent songwriting talent. He wrote the bulk of the song back in their Troubadour days, and his trademark heartwrenching vocal style is already evident: especially on the bridge. With Michael Clarke on bongos, this was the sound of the birth of The Byrds, and is their best-known song that wasn't originally officially released. Compared to the tracks on their debut album, it's very sentimental, but the commercial potential of this early West Coast sound was clearly realised in The Turtles' version. Publishing-wise, it remains McGuinn and Clark's highest-grossing song.

'The Reason Why' (Clark)

This is one of the more-creamy-sounding *Preflyte* tracks, with an already distinctive McGuinn guitar break. Elsewhere the Everly-influenced harmonies are quite raw, and it sounds like prototype garage-band pop from 1964, with a bit of Bo Diddley thrown in. While it certainly gives clues as to where The Byrds' sound was going, Clark eventually wrote stronger material. The lyric comes across as a bit angsty – certainly, his lyric depth matured within a year, and much stronger songs of his did make the album. But there's no denying that Clark's emotive and contemplative vocal style is taking shape here: an early example of even better things to come.

'For Me Again' (Clark)

It says something that they could ignore this for their debut, as it's one of the best unreleased Clark songs from the time. It could be argued that its potential isn't quite fulfilled by the end. If they'd taken more time, it could've been augmented with stronger harmonies and a fuller guitar sound, though the glorious bridge is already perfect.

The lyric finds Clark using metaphors for love by referencing the seasons and weather. While it's easy to see how they could afford to leave this off the album when their material was becoming stronger, it's still stronger than some of the debut's weaker songs.

'Boston' (Clark)

With its plodding bass line, this now sounds dated – like a parody of a mid-1960s folk rock band trying to do Chuck Berry. It was never going to be considered for inclusion on the album, and was just something they could play live until they had more songs in their repertoire.

'You Movin'' (Clark)

The Wrecking Crew's Larry Knechtel and Hal Blaine were on bass and drums, respectively, here, and there's also a Johnny Rivers influence. Some of Clark's phrasing is similar to that of Rivers, where there's a lineage to the phrasing of R.E.M's Michael Stipe too. Again, like 'Boston', it's derivative, but it gallops along, and they loved playing it live to wind up the Ciro's crowd into freaky dancing.

'Airport Song' (Crosby, McGuinn)

This was inspired by the days the band spent watching planes land at LAX, and features Clark on harmonica. Crosby's first lead vocal is striking here, and the smooth groove pointed towards his later jazz-like arrangements – early evidence that he could become the band's secret songwriting weapon. You can certainly hear where he'd go with his jazz-inflected ballads on this one.

'Tomorrow is a Long Ways Away' (Clark, Crosby, McGuinn)

Though some critics referred to this as a revelatory outtake when it was first released on the 1988 *In The Beginning* compilation, it's a bit dated and dirgelike in either acoustic or electric form. Clark was writing better songs than this by the time of the debut album, though, admittedly, this attempt at Elizabethan balladry was an example of his growing confidence as a songwriter.

Another track with Michael Clarke on bongos, it was felt that Gene's voice was too deep and had too much vibrato (particularly evident on the bridge) to be considered for inclusion on the debut. The electric version isn't too different, but enough for Crosby and McGuinn to gain writing credits.

'The Only Girl I Adore' (Crosby, McGuinn)

This was an embryo of the Beatles/folk combination that The Byrds were to perfect by 1965. Complete with 'yeah yeah' refrains, there's a decent early-McCartney-sounding song in there, save for the dodgy Liverpool backing vocal accents. There's also an Everly Brothers influence, especially the harmonies. The rhythm guitar part, too, is pure Don Everly – a common theme in early Crosby songs.

However, this unplugged-Beatles-sounding track (which features on the 1970 Together Records *Early LA* compilation, along with a different mix of 'You Movin'' and two David Crosby demos), sounds like The Jet Set in their infancy, and by the time of its recording, the band had moved on to a fuller sound.

'Do You Believe in Magic' (Sebastian)
This cover of the Lovin' Spoonful song was released as a single for Record Store Day 2017, and is disposable, to say the least. It was recorded for a *Hullabaloo* TV appearance, where it was used to introduce the guests. You can see it on YouTube. For completists only.

Afterword
The album was a game changer that helped invent a new musical genre, and spawned a guitar sound that's still heard today – 'Mr. Tambourine Man' defining the folk rock genre more than any other song. Folk and rock were no longer mutually exclusive, and The Byrds demonstrated that it was possible to have creative freedom *and* a hit. Jim Dickson had told them to seek substance and depth, and to record something people would still listen to in 40 years. Try 58 years and counting! Five young Americans had made folk fab, and were already working on their follow-up while riding the crest of a wave.

Turn! Turn! Turn! (1965)

Personnel:
Jim McGuinn: 12-string guitar, vocals
Gene Clark: tambourine, vocals
David Crosby: rhythm guitar, vocals
Chris Hillman: bass, vocals
Michael Clarke: drums
Producer: Terry Melcher
Record label: Columbia, CBS (UK)
Release date: 6 December 1965
Chart position: UK: 11, US 17
Running time: 30:24

The Byrds began recording their follow-up album a week after *Mr. Tambourine Man* had reached the shops, and the two were released only six months apart. This was not an uncommon schedule in the 1960s: remember, the Beatles' canon was recorded in a little under seven years.

The Byrds were now popular with adoring teenage fans, and were receiving masses of radio airplay, with their faces now commonplace in teen magazines. Their dress sense also entered the zeitgeist, with their images used to represent the new groovy aspects of the growing counterculture. McGuinn's Benjamin Franklin-style granny glasses and David Crosby's green cape were imitated – their look appeared on US sitcoms like *The Munsters*, to illustrate the hip new teenage look. The Byrds had changed the Sunset Strip, and the dance floor at Ciro's was now a madhouse. A hardcore of followers – pop-art painters, bearded sculptors and groovy scenesters (including a young Kim Fowley) – suddenly taught Hollywood to dance again. The Byrds were now the pied pipers to the new generation of L.A. bands, and the whole demographic bridge between beats and hippies is best presented by what was happening on the Strip. It seemed like every mid-1960s Hollywood movie that needed a nightclub scene used Ciros' crowd as a guide.

Meanwhile, Derek Taylor had left his Beatles press-officer role, became The Byrds publicist and quickly organised a 1965 UK tour. Unfortunately, this was overhyped, especially with the band constantly labelled as 'America's Beatles'. A mix of poor sound and the band's aloof stage presence prompted almost unilateral criticism in the UK press. Huddling for lengthy discussions about what to play next, certainly took its toll in robbing their performances of any momentum. 'Flopsville', cried *Melody Maker*, referring to how they tuned up for five minutes behind a curtain before getting slow applause.

Admittedly, for all their non-conformist California cool, The Byrds had a detachment about them. They weren't used to the UK club scene, were too stoic on stage, and were seen as remote as they seemed to have little warmth when interviewed. Even John Peel had referred to them as unpleasant when he met them in autumn 1965 but did concede that their aloof cool was probably the way L.A. bands had to be. McGuinn later admitted it wasn't intended to be an affront to the audience by being incommunicative; it was simply that the band expected their music to do the talking.

However, the tour heightened the band's relationship with The Beatles, who voiced their approval of The Byrds, acknowledging them as creative allies. By the time of the new album's release in their homeland, The Byrds were regarded as one of popular music's vanguards, along with The Beatles, Bob Dylan, The Beach Boys and The Rolling Stones.

They secured appearances on every American TV show, from *Hullabaloo* to *Shindig*, and *The Ed Sullivan Show* would follow in the autumn. In contrast to their live reputation in the UK, their studio sound couldn't have been more different: soft, warm and incandescent.

Similar in structure to their debut, *Turn! Turn! Turn!* included a mix of originals, folk standards and Dylan covers. Gene Clark's songs were some of the best of the folk rock genre, and the band began to transcend their influences. But though the album included one of their all-time calling cards and some strong Clark originals, in retrospect, it seems like a tired offspring of their debut – lacking its fullness and punch. Side two certainly suffers from second-album fatigue, and some of the B-sides and outtakes would've been better album choices.

The album sessions had not been without tension. As well as band politics – mainly to do with songwriting opportunities – friction had developed between the producer Melcher and manager Dickson. He was critical of Melcher's production, and wanted to produce the band himself. Also, Melcher and Crosby didn't like each other. Crosby felt that Melcher didn't want his songs on the records, which fuelled further tensions. There were also issues with Gene Clark. Though at this stage, he was the band's only consistently decent writer (Crosby later referred to him as the heart and soul of the original Byrds), Clark was a fragile soul, and fame with all its trappings didn't sit easily with him.

Released in December 1965, *Turn! Turn! Turn!* received decent reviews, and critics agreed it was inferior to their debut. *Melody Maker* rightly commented that it wouldn't sell as much as *Mr. Tambourine Man*, but was immensely enjoyable. Portentously, McGuinn confirmed in a *Melody Maker* interview that though they were keen on all contemporary music, they didn't care for labels!

The album cover shows the group sitting with studied cool and aloof 1960s attitude. McGuinn appears to be wearing a Dickensian double-breasted suit, while Clark and Hillman looked so non-plussed about everything, and Clarke never looked more like Brian Jones: they all exuded California cool. In 2013, Crosby auctioned off his trademark suede cape seen on the sleeve, fetching in excess of $15,000. In the sleeve notes, Derek Taylor made the most of his Beatles connections, commenting on how much they liked The Byrds, and included praise from The Beatles themselves.

Like the debut album, *Turn! Turn! Turn!* was about to have a US number 1 with its title track. In early-1965, the group poised to become America's answer to The Beatles was Paul Revere & The Raiders, but by late-1965 The Byrds made protest songs sound like love songs, on waves of electric guitars, and were the only new American band to have two US number 1s in that giddy year. They'd released a year's worth of music that, by most band's stature would've sufficed as their career's work. For all the emerging tension, *Mr. Tambourine Man* and *Turn! Turn! Turn!* remain the definitive folk-rock albums. Their sound was like a radiant sunlight reflected through speakers.

'Turn! Turn! Turn! (To Everything There Is a Season)' (Adapted, Music by Pete Seeger)

The band had intended to release a version of Dylan's 'It's All Over Now, Baby Blue' as their third single, but instead decided on the song based on a popular English folk song called 'To Everything There is a Season', which McGuinn had previously arranged in a chamber-folk style for *Judy Collins 3*. That arrangement was similar, but McGuinn eventually refashioned the song into a gripping 1960s anthem sung in a hipster drawl. With more emphasis on the melody, he added some elegant arpeggios and jazzed-up the arrangement with a rock and samba rhythm. This transcending version took 78 takes to record, but it became one of the greatest recordings of their career.

Pete Seeger originally adapted it from the *Bible*, adding his own melody and the lines 'A time of peace/I swear it's not too late'. The Byrds' version moved Seeger enough that he changed his arrangement in future performances, and McGuinn still has the note Seeger sent the group, saying he loved their version. It's ironic to think that Seeger would get kudos (and royalty cheques) for an electric folk-rock hit after (allegedly) threatening to pull the plug on Dylan's blasphemous electric set at Newport that year!

The establishment who'd previously ridiculed rock 'n' roll, now realised what some of the youth culture was trying to convey, presumably because they could sense it was profitable – and in that sense, 'Turn! Turn! Turn!' was groundbreaking. Pop culture effectively welcomed a song that included passages dating from the *Bible* and with probably the oldest lyric in the history of rock 'n' roll. Thought to have been written approximately 1000 years before the birth of Christ, the song was banned as blasphemous in South Africa, as the message had been sabotaged by a rock rhythm!

With a changed chord structure and a Phil Spector rhythm to make it more danceable, they uplifted the song by extending the melody with title refrains – sung with a dash of the eerie – while respecting the song's message. The Byrds' version has a flowing arpeggio, with McGuinn applying a rolling banjo technique to the Rickenbacker, and the opening riff – suggested by Crosby – creates circles around the bass line. Then there's Michael Clarke's samba drumming, and of course, those new-age Gregorian-toned harmonies starting each verse's prayer and coaxing out the joyous chorus. The song's progression from mournful folk to a sparkly folk rock anthem is one of the greatest examples of the acoustic and electric worlds merging. The Byrds' arrangement helped challenge standard three-chord radio pop with a sound that's permeated rock music ever since.

Crosby felt it was a great poem with an unpretentious message, while Hillman still regards it as the quintessential signature Byrds song, and their most iconic in terms of capturing the vibes of the mid-1960s. The track has been used in lots of films – most famously in *Forrest Gump* (1994). It also resonated with the US public in 1965 in the wake of the growing unpopularity of the US involvement in Vietnam. By the mid-to-late 1960s, popular music connected with both the protest and counterculture movements, and this song became a subversive anthem for the anti-war movement.

Though Dylan's 'Like a Rolling Stone' had paved the way for longer singles that summer, 3m:40s was still a long song in 1965. But it didn't stop 'Turn! Turn! Turn!' from reaching number 1 in America at the end of 1965. It eventually became their biggest-selling single, but didn't do as well in the UK, where George Harrison said he felt sorry for the people who didn't buy it.

The socially conscious content of the chosen Dylan originals and traditional folk songs were having a profound influence on the evolution of popular music, by bringing a literal sense to mainstream rock 'n' roll. Musician and writer Sid Griffin thinks the track encapsulates a beautiful 1960s moment, and always feels 'warm and positive' when he hears it. It's hard to disagree. Try listening to McGuinn's guitar break without feeling it represents the high point of the mid-1960s when it briefly seemed possible to change the world through pop music. That probably sounds twee and naïve now, but this must've seemed epochal in 1965.

When everyone contributed equally and played with one mind, The Byrds were unbeatable. McGuinn confirms it was just a standard folk song, but by the time he rearranged it, it came out as rock 'n' roll. He felt as if he was programmed to do that back then.

Byrdfact – the version of 'Turn! Turn! Turn!' in the 1990 box set where the vocals are panned to the left and instruments to the right is slightly longer.

'It Won't Be Wrong' (McGuinn, Gerst)

This is a much-more-passionate version than the original, which had been released as 'Don't Be Long' on the B-side of the Beefeaters single. McGuinn felt the earlier Beatlesque take deserved a rebirth, so he added fuller harmonies and a sparkling guitar sound. The new driving rhythm, with its dramatic tempo changes, was a stirring example of how much the band had progressed musically in a year.

When 'Set You Free This Time' struggled as a single, Columbia flipped it over and made this the A-side. However, though the band loved the new production, it only reached 63 on the US charts. The confusion regarding

A-side status didn't help sales or airplay, and it inevitably paled as a single when compared to its glorious predecessor.

But the song positively chimes from its intro, with stronger harmonies and less whiny vocals. The bridge in particular, works so much better here, and the most remarkable thing is the guitar pattern running throughout: is that the sound of raga guitar runs in their infancy?

'Set You Free This Time' (Clark)
This is the album's most astonishing original track, with Clark's most sophisticated and dense lyric so far. Exuding bitterness and retribution, he was now clearly influenced by Dylan. The intricate subject matter probably divulges more about Clark's fragile state – his new songs were not in the tradition of popular love songs by 1965 standards but were more mature. It was sung with a pained and meek vocal, lending the album an emotional character, and he seems to slow down near the end, emphasising the melancholia. It's like an elegy for a dying relationship – the majestic guitars are a lovely contrast to the mournful lyric, and the harmonica-led fade-out is gorgeous.

Gene Clark wrote the song on the British tour after a night out drinking with Paul McCartney and various Animals members at the Scotch of St. James club in London; Clark claiming he wrote it in a couple of hours. But he was upset with the band's attitude when recording it, as they left the studio before he'd finished his vocals.

The track was released as a single in January 1966, but its dense lyric and slow tempo probably contributed to it only reaching 63 on the *Billboard* chart and failing to reach the UK chart at all. Obviously, record buyers weren't used to heartbreaking folk-rock ballads being so elegant.

An interesting footnote is the BBC apparently contributing money to the production of a promo film that was never made. But the band did perform the song on the US show *Where The Action Is*, which was Clark's last TV appearance with the original Byrds.

'Lay Down Your Weary Tune' (Dylan)
An unused song from Bob Dylan's *The Times They Are a-Changin'* album, this gentle and mournful rendition is a bit weary and nondescript, and is crying out for a Rickenbacker solo. But what do I know? – it's apparently the cover that convinced Dylan that the group really had something and weren't just imitating. This slow, melancholy take is almost hymnlike with a dreary McGuinn arrangement. The harmonies are well sung (including Hillman's first vocals for The Byrds), but the drum fills throughout seem inappropriate for an elegy-like rendition. Melcher was not a fan of the production either, feeling the track was too monotonous. But some fans think the criticisms are misplaced and that the lamenting feel perfectly suits an album also including an elegy for a recently assassinated president (see next track).

It's intriguing that Gene Clark later borrowed some key chorus lines for 'Strength of Strings' on his 1974 *No Other* album.

'He Was a Friend of Mine' (Trad: additional lyrics by McGuinn)

This traditional folk ballad was moulded into a eulogy for John F. Kennedy, and was apparently written on the night of 22 November 1963. Bob Dylan had also previously demoed this, with a different lyric. The Byrds changed the melody slightly, and in fairness, probably made the tune more palatable for commercial audiences, with the chorus vocal stretched to accentuate the melody. However, Crosby wasn't keen on the tambourine part or the Mellotron chords throughout the song, which he claims Melcher added without asking them.

I hate to disagree with Croz, but I think the part adds a nice layer to the arrangement.

It now sounds sweet but dated. The anachronistic lyric is forgivable, as the effect of Kennedy's assassination was still being felt, even two years after his death. The song was always an audience favourite, and a demo single was actually pressed and sent to DJs, but was never picked up on. The band infamously performed the song at Monterey in 1967 – when Crosby had his onstage rant about the failings of the Warren Commission's findings on JFK's assassination.

'The World Turns all Around Her' (Clark)

Another tortured Gene Clark love song of longing and loss, he simply had a pop sensibility the rest of the band couldn't match. It's one of his finest compositions, and one of the best singles the band never released! It's a romping proto-power-pop classic, and the harmonies are among the album's best. Indeed it probably would've been a better single than 'It Won't Be Wrong'. Clark always loved the fast electric arrangement, where it sounds like a companion to 'Feel a Whole Lot Better'.

Crosby regularly joked that Clark's complicated love life meant that anytime he broke up with someone, they always got a great song. The lyric is certainly related to 'Set You Free This Time'. Who knows what influenced his more sensitive lyrics, but what *is* clear is that while there were many ways of expressing free love in the mid-1960s, Clark seems less crude and more sophisticated. It's a good example of how a sad song could successfully include a rock rhythm without negating the romantic envy rhetoric.

Byrdfact – the alternate version in the 1990 box set and CD reissue had added bongos.

'Satisfied Mind' (Hayes, Rhodes)

An early flirtation with Nashville, this was the band's first tentative foray into country, and foreshadowed things to come. Hillman had previously tried to bring country songs into their repertoire, but Crosby always objected.

Though the song was first popularised by country singer Porter Wagoner, Hillman was more inspired by his love of the Hamilton Camp version. The Byrds applied their folk rock template to this melancholy ballad, which is arranged as a folk dirge. It's also probably fair to say that they were deferring to the lyric's rejection of materialism: something the emerging hippie culture was enthusiastic about.

The Byrds' first journey into country music is quite tepid and probably a lost opportunity for Hillman to take his first lead vocal (McGuinn's voice is most prominent in the harmonies). The band had suggested McGuinn sing it, as, though Hillman had moaned about his small role in the recording session, he didn't have the confidence to take the lead. Yet.

'If You're Gone' (Clark)

Gene Clark had the ability to write something heartfelt, even when the song didn't particularly possess an engaging melody. Here, McGuinn also offers a sombre tone, to complement the darker aspects of Clark's doleful folk-rock power ballad.

While McGuinn's guitar line is fantastic, the backing vocals are the real stars here, with McGuinn's unusual harmonic blend giving the song a sense of melancholy similar to that of The Kinks on 'See My Friends'. He added a vocal harmony drone in 5ths to create an eerie Gregorian effect. The drone added depth, highlighting the sorrowful tone, and showed the band could vary their background harmonies.

The sound was engaging and innovative. Mid-1960s pop songs rarely had this level of tasteful pathos, and in Clark's album contributions, you can hear the influence the band had on the likes of Big Star and The Go-Betweens.

'The Times They Are a-Changin'' (Dylan)

This sounds so calculated that it comes across as sarcastic. McGuinn sounds full of vitriol, while Clarke's crashing cymbals seem out of place. They actually recorded a radically different but much more convincing arrangement during an appearance on *Hullabaloo* in November 1965. That performance was scheduled to be released as a single, as they'd hoped Melcher would polish it, but it didn't happen. So they cancelled it and considered a cover of 'It's All Over Now Baby Blue', before eventually opting for 'Turn! Turn! Turn!'. However, CBS in the UK *did* issue an EP with this album version as the lead track.

This version is brash and bright enough but uninspired. It's too fast and one of their least successful Dylan covers. A lack of sincerity gives it a disingenuous feel. The harmonies and guitar sound are crisp, but ultimately the track sounds tame. The CD reissue includes the *Hullabaloo* take, which is much better – more upbeat with more-flexible vocals. But for all the band's dislike of this released version, it was an important catalyst for them writing more original material.

'Wait and See' (McGuinn, Crosby)

This first McGuinn/Crosby writing collaboration is Byrds-by-numbers. Crosby later couldn't recall the extent of his contribution, and it's probably the album's weakest song. Maybe this was included to break up the Gene Clark songs that McGuinn and Crosby felt were monopolising the publishing royalties?

It's catchy enough, and the backing is lively. Though the guitar break is pure, blissful 1965 Byrds, it's a sideways step compared to the debut material. It's strange if it was a compromise to put it on the album, since Crosby's 'Stranger in a Strange Land' was more hip, and if it wasn't because of the number of Clark songs getting on the albums, then his 'The Day Walk' is a more interesting option too.

'Oh! Susannah' (Foster, Arranged by McGuinn)

This rocked-up rejig of a 19th-century Stephen Foster minstrel sing-along closes the album in inventive but ultimately throwaway fashion. McGuinn tried to transform it into a definitive Byrds cover by speeding it up and replacing banjo with electric guitar. Michael Clarke came up with the playful military drumming (used to better effect here than on the original World Pacific version of 'Mr. Tambourine Man').

This was another track chosen instead of 'Stranger in a Strange Land', but even McGuinn later admitted he was unhappy with it. Though Bob Dylan had wanted them to cut it as a humorous track, it's a failed attempt at humour. However, Jim Dickson thought there was ironic hip 1960s humour in there, and suggested to Columbia that Miles Davis should perform the Stephen Foster songbook as some sort of caustic comment on racism.

Anyway, while listening to the song now suggests a twee, lightweight end to the album, it's the kind of giddy plunge into folk-hued country music that The Byrds later undertook in their groundbreaking country-rock work.

Connected Flights
'She Don't Care About Time' (Clark)

The 'Turn! Turn! Turn!' B-side earned Clark enough royalties to buy a Porsche! It would've probably been a hit if released as an A-side, and it beggars belief why it wasn't included on the album. It's glorious and rightly appears on most Byrds compilations.

The driving rhythm carries Clark's Dylanesque lyric along for the Rickenbacker ride, sounding like a trippy medieval festival song. It's one of those early Byrds classics where all the band contribute something: for once, they were like a gang in unison. McGuinn's guitar break again alludes to Bach's 'Jesu, Joy of Man's Desiring', and was recorded with two of the Beatles in attendance. While George Harrison admitted that The Beatles' 'If I Needed Someone' took the riff from 'The Bells of Rhymney', he later wrote to Derek Taylor confessing that it also took the drum part from 'She Don't Care About

Time'. By 1965, The Beatles and Dylan were leaning towards each other in concept, but now The Byrds were influencing both.

The influence of Dylan's lyric is obvious here, with reference to Clark's love being somewhere on the 'end of time', and the chorus phrasing – again, much admired by Harrison – suggested a band full of confidence in the studio.

The single version is best. Another mix on the CD reissue and the *Cancelled Flights* box has a harmonica solo accompanying McGuinn's solo. There's also an '(I Can't Get No) Satisfaction'-type piano riff played by Melcher on that earlier version. But this mix doesn't really work – why partly hide McGuinn's glorious guitar break with a harmonica break far too high in the mix? Thankfully, the instrumental portions of either mix failed to compromise those glorious vocals.

A nice footnote is that a shiny new version appeared on Chris Hillman's 2017 album *Biding My Time*.

'It's All Over Now, Baby Blue' (Dylan)

This is included here because the definitive Byrds' version is this supercharged take, and not the tired version on the *Ballad of Easy Rider* album four years later.

This version was cut without Melcher, and was readied as a single since a master and label matrix were assigned, signalling imminent release. In late summer 1965 at a Columbia Records convention, the song was even introduced as the forthcoming Byrds single. It was later withdrawn, as momentum was gathering on the commercial potential of their timeless version of 'Turn! Turn! Turn!'. However, this version of 'It's All Over Now, Baby Blue' appeared on *Never Before*, and *Cancelled Flights:* the 2004 box set of cancelled Byrds singles. They also cut a 'Version 1', which appears on the 2000 *Sanctuary* outtakes album, but the general feel and vocals are better on this version.

The choice to not release it wasn't supposed to be seen as a slight on their version, but was because they didn't want to merely be seen as a cover band. Well, that's one reason. Another was down to politics – by now, Dickson wanted to produce the band, and *he* actually cut this version. In the meantime, Melcher had tried to cut a version without Crosby and Clark.

Either way, it's a great version. McGuinn's vocal (and the backing vocals) are more-breezy, and there's great tangled guitar runs with a killer Rickenbacker solo. Clarke's drumming is also great, and the McGuinn/Clark/Crosby harmonies are so warm, especially when compared to the lame 1969 take. But it could be argued that they miss the bitterness at the song's heart, and McGuinn later claimed he hated it even more than their version of 'The Times They Are a-Changin'. But deep down, he was probably fed up with covering Dylan.

'The Day Walk (Never Before)' (Clark)

This was the last song Clark recorded during his first stint with The Byrds. The subtitle gave their 1987 rarities set its title (introducing fans to Byrds outtakes for the first time).

The track points to where his solo career was to go in the next few years, and it's a crime it didn't appear on the *Turn! Turn! Turn!* album. It's a much better option than 'Wait and See', and the Dylanesque lyric has an ambiguous quality that would've given the album a certain amount of mystery.

Clarke's drumming is a highlight, and with Hillman's swaggering bass line, it almost sounds funky by 1965 folk-rock standards. McGuinn's guitar pattern running counterpoint to Clark's mysterious lyric, works well.

One of the highlights of the *Never Before* album, there's always a tinge of 'what might've been if Gene had stayed' sadness when listening to this.

'Stranger in a Strange Land' (Crosby)

This title was taken from the science fiction novel by Robert A. Heinlein. It's really a backing track, but you can already hear its potential. A vocal version was released by Blackburn & Snow, though they used Crosby's pseudonym Samuel F. Omar for the writing credit. Around this time, Crosby was employing Heinlein's concepts and vocabulary in Byrds magazine interviews, but he got little support from the band to record this or include it on the album. In later years, Crosby claimed it wasn't a particularly good song. Though written two years before the Summer of Love, he felt it was a naïve comment on the hippie ethos.

However, The Byrds' instrumental version has merit and is an interesting cut. There's more cyclical guitar work from McGuinn, and – most significantly – Clarke's drumming really drives the track, alongside a funky bass line.

Afterword

The rate of change in 1960s music meant that by the time of this album's release in late-1965, The Byrds were already a bit predictable and tired as a live act. The rest of America had caught up with the folk rock sound by then, but The Byrds were already moving on. Saleswise they'd peaked, but creatively they were just starting. While Columbia's mantra was now 'folk + rock = profits', the band's timeless slices of bittersweet pop would make way for their new obsessions. Looking to expand their sound, and influenced by Gene Clark's songwriting successes, McGuinn and Crosby began pushing their own songwriting.

Interlude: Stranger Than Known

Though McGuinn, Crosby and Hillman would evolve as songwriters, by December 1965, things were unsettled for The Byrds. They'd already revolutionised American pop but were looking to change. After a poorly-received UK visit, no group-written hit single, internal friction and Gene Clark's unsettled nature, where would the next flight go? Enter a folk ballad Clark wrote about that fateful UK tour.

They had taken speed to keep up with schedules and grass to chill out, but Crosby had now introduced the band to LSD. Long bus (and acid) trips now had the soundtrack of Crosby's tapes of Ravi Shankar's Indian ragas and John Coltrane's free jazz. These gradually informed the next masterpiece in The Byrds' repertoire. McGuinn and Crosby particularly wanted to create new sounds and inform new directions. By the time this musical gumbo of innovation had touched down, the band had invented a new musical language.

Fifth Dimension (1966)

Personnel:
Jim McGuinn: 12 string guitar, vocals
David Crosby: rhythm guitar, vocals
Chris Hillman: bass, vocals
Michael Clarke: drums
Gene Clark: tambourine, harmonica, vocals
Van Dyke Parks: keyboards
Producer: Allen Stanton
Record label: Columbia, CBS (UK)
Release date: 18 July 1966
Chart position: UK: 27, US: 24
Running time: 29:59

Within a month of the *Turn! Turn! Turn!'* release, Crosby and Dickson
persuaded McGuinn to replace Terry Melcher. Though Columbia's Allen
Stanton was listed as the next album's producer, the band effectively
produced it, as Stanton was an A&R man who spent most of his time reading
the newspaper, as he didn't understand The Byrds or their music. While
he read his paper, the band – now feeling stuck in a folk-rock box – leapt
forward at a dazzling pace.

The band had recorded a new song called 'Eight Miles High', but Columbia
refused to release it due to it being recorded at RCA studios. So, the band
re-recorded it and it was released as a single in March 1966. The song was
a huge creative leap forward and is considered crucial in transforming folk
rock into the new psychedelic sound. From the opening pumping rumbling
bass line to McGuinn's frenzied guitar solo, it took its inspiration from John
Coltrane and Ravi Shankar. But with the single's release, the band suffered
its first serious setback, as 'Eight Miles High' was banned from radio playlists
due to its apparent drug connotations. This will be discussed in more detail in
this chapter, but it was already clear that The Byrds were struggling to remain
a hitmaking entity – not only through drug-reference accusations, but with
their music's increasing transitional nature.

Now they had an even bigger setback to overcome: the departure of Gene
Clark. The official reason was – ironically – his fear of flying. He had a panic
attack on a New York plane, and disembarked before it took off. McGuinn
famously told him, 'If you can't fly, you can't be a Byrd!'. But Clark also
left partly due to the tension around his songwriting income making him
the wealthiest Byrds member, and an increasing unease with his newfound
fame. Jim Dickson later confessed that he'd planned to spin Clark off as a
folk-rock Elvis.

Clark left a distinctive songwriting legacy, but the band learnt throughout
their career to regroup quickly and successfully. Unlike future changes, this
didn't involve a new face, and the band continued as a quartet. Most bands

never recover from the loss of their main creative source, but The Byrds were keen to enter the vacuum Clark left. More pressure was bestowed on McGuinn and Crosby, who were forced to mature as writers. To fill the Clark vocal gap, Hillman joined in the vocal harmonies, while McGuinn and Crosby were both comfortable taking the lead.

The new material heralded a more intelligent and ambitious sound, with explorations into raga and improvisation. While they emulated the sounds of the sitar and Coltrane on a 12-string, they were still influencing and being influenced by The Beatles – both musically and in lifestyle choices. It was evident that drugs were becoming more prevalent in pop culture. In 1965, marijuana was the prevalent drug of choice, but by 1966, groups were using psychedelics more, which was influencing the music.

While the *Fifth Dimension* album continued the previous album's trend of mixing innovative genius with half-baked filler, its most innovative parts contained more groundbreaking psychedelia. Tracks like '5D' and 'I See You' revealed The Byrds as pioneers of folk to freak out, with 'Eight Miles High' as the marker. Again, other acts looked to The Byrds as pioneers to conquer new worlds. A lot of the London underground scene was listening to Los Angeles music in 1966. If London was twinned with anywhere in 1966, it was L.A. Syd Barrett (Pink Floyd), in particular, spent a lot of 1966 listening to Love's debut and the *Fifth Dimension* album. Bands like The Yardbirds and Tomorrow (featuring future Yes guitarist Steve Howe) were obviously listening, while Cream's 'Dance The Night Away' borrowed directly from 'Eight Miles High' in its guitar-solo crescendo. Ironically, The Byrds had left the preppy folk scene because of British versions of American music, but were now influencing the British scene themselves. Acts like The Move featured lots of Byrds covers, and Fairport Convention had a Byrds influence in their early repertoire, such as their acid-drenched version of 'Reno Nevada'. Leader Ashley Hutchings was excited by The Byrds' innovations, and to him it was natural for a rock band to explore its own culture of folk music.

The San Francisco scene especially transformed the emerging counterculture, taking The Byrds' flight path to write about their LSD experiences: such as 'Bass Strings' by Country Joe and the Fish. The Byrds' eastern scales could be heard in emerging guitarists like Jefferson Airplane's Jorma Kaukonen and Quicksilver Messenger Service' John Cipollina, where they added a drone feel and took the sound to new sonic spaces. Peter Lewis from Moby Grape described hearing The Byrds innovations as an epiphany – mixing folk music with blues and jazz opened up new avenues, and informed that band's classic, eclectic debut album, bound with electric guitars and three-part harmonies. Another Byrds' influence on bands like Jefferson Airplane and Moby Grape was that they now had multiple songwriters.

In New York, even Lou Reed (who despised psychedelia) liked The Byrds – especially McGuinn's guitar sound on 'Eight Miles High' – and was clearly influenced by McGuinn's guitar drones. In L.A., The Doors used John

Coltrane's versions of 'My Favourite Things' and 'Olé' to inform the middle instrumental section of 'Light My Fire', just as The Byrds themselves were experimenting and jamming on a new improvised piece based on Miles Davis' 'Milestones'. (There is 1966 rehearsal footage on YouTube.)

The Byrds were taking the erudite sound of 'Mr. Tambourine Man' into a new age, with challenging and more-free musical structures. *Fifth Dimension* continued their tradition of restless-yet-accessible experimentation. Track for track, it's not as strong as their debut or as good as the next two albums, but it still works as an ambitious song collection. Lots of bands now wanted to test the boundaries as a consequence of some of this album's songs. Remember, this was still only mid-1966!

It's largely 'Eight Miles High's' presence that ensures the album is always granted a positive response. Had they produced another track of similar ambition, it would've guaranteed the album classic status.

The album received largely favourable reviews, though it sold less than the first two. *Melody Maker* declared it sounded like the band were standing on a cloud surrounded by wisps of vapour, while San Francisco's *Mojo Navigator* said every song was flavoured with originality. The cover was striking, and the first to include The Byrds' psychedelic mosaic logo. It's one of the grooviest of far-out 1960s album sleeves, with all four members perched on a magic carpet.

While the album was admittedly front-loaded and runs out of steam on side two, at its best, it was ahead of most other artists, and for some, this is where psychedelia started. In less than a year, they went from 'Mr. Tambourine Man' to 'Eight Miles High': a giant leap forward. The three albums The Byrds recorded in 1966 and 1967 are sometimes referred to as their Holy Trinity. Those mid-1960s classics – which took the band from being folk rock harbingers to psychedelic and country-rock pioneers – are probably unequalled by any contemporary American band in their field. The sublime combination of folk rock and experimental acid rock starts here.

'5D (Fifth Dimension)' (McGuinn)

Continuing McGuinn's obsession with science fiction, this was also banned by some US radio stations when released as a single, for its lyric allegedly promoting drug use. It's a great opening track, where an ethereal drone is married to a jig, creating an acid-drenched sea shanty.

McGuinn came up with the waltz-time rhythm that should've been too square to work as it was out of place with the era. But it works perfectly, thanks in no small way to his inventive layered guitar and the band's ravishing harmonies, which perfectly fit the floating music. Listen to the last vocal part where Crosby hits that harmony: perfect! Clarke's drums and Hillman's bass runs also provide momentum. The arrangement is decorated with Van Dyke Parks' haunting organ chords, where he was instructed by McGuinn to 'Think Bach'.

Drugs are playfully implicit, and the abstract Dylanesque lyric suggests this was a long way from the previous year's folk rock, with references to two-dimensional boundaries. Lines like 'And I will remember the place that is now/That has ended before the beginning' were not your average mid-1960s lyrics. McGuinn was dealing with Einstein's theory of relativity and the unspecified fifth dimension. It was essentially a poem written to a pendulum rhythm about the Don Landis book *1-2-3-4, More, More, More, More*, where the fifth dimension is perceived as a void in space where time has no meaning. With drugs already inspiring folk rock's next phase, McGuinn said he dropped acid to try to understand the universe better and to inform the song's theme. He saw it as a spiritual song inspired by Islam, rather than an acid-drenched drug song. Whatever the intention, some of its philosophies anticipated the emerging flower-power movement.

Ultimately, the attempt to make a hit single about the infinite beyond, failed. Though by the time of its release, The Byrds had morphed into a different band with new objectives. Their audacity in the studio was now dwarfing their interest in the hitmaking process – with the exception of Michael Clarke and – of course – the record label. For a pop single in 1966, this was cerebral.

'Wild Mountain Thyme' (Trad. Arranged by McGuinn, Crosby, Hillman, Clarke)

While The Byrds explored new frontiers, they remained faithful to their folk roots with this staple of the coffee-house circuit. This harmony-rich arrangement of Robert Tannahill's 18th-century Scottish folk tale 'The Braes of Balquhidder' saw all four Byrds receive a publishing credit for their arrangement. McGuinn had already rearranged this as a soloist at the Troubadour in the early-1960s, playing it on a five-string banjo. The Byrds added a romantic orchestrated twist, giving the song less of an ethnic feel. Producer Allen Stanton suggested the strings – one of his few contributions – and they sound tasteful and sensitive, further evidence for this being the version on *Another Dimension* (a 10" vinyl release of *Fifth Dimension* outtakes) with no string overdubs, and poorer for it.

This interpretation manages to blend folky cowboy and Eastern raga. Those instinctive sunny harmonies and upbeat drums produce a merry, dreamy slant on a sad old folk ballad. The blissful harmonies were partly inspired by Crosby's love of female harmonies in Bulgarian folk music. Unlike their more traditional readings of old folk songs, this feels like it's being transported into another world. The instrumental break with the hummed vocal line is absolutely sublime.

'Mr. Spaceman' (McGuinn)

Forget *Sweetheart of The Rodeo*, this is where cosmic country rock started for The Byrds. We'd already had theories of relativity, and now alien visitations were playfully discussed, accompanied by a goofy, cosmic, upbeat country two-step. Yes, it's only 1966 and they're already working toward their next pioneering sound.

This whimsical tale about friendly space aliens became a minor hit single and has gained a certain importance in The Byrds' career arc as being a specific reference point for the Hillman-influenced country vibe on the follow-up album *Younger Than Yesterday*, let alone *Sweetheart*'s country-rock path. It was partly inspired by The Beatles' country riffs on *Beatles for Sale* – such as 'Baby's in Black': their Everly Brothers-influenced country song. However tongue-in-cheek it might sound, McGuinn was genuinely intrigued with adding a space theme to a country song with a tidy guitar solo. He originally intended to write a more-serious song, but as it took shape, it became more playful – like bluegrass folk cowboys mutating into space cowboys (loosely the concept of future Byrds album *Dr. Byrds & Mr. Hyde*).

A genuine attempt by McGuinn to make contact with alien life forms, the song's experimentation did find kinship with some of the growing counterculture. Though not necessarily one of the album's best tracks (it now sounds a tad too whimsical), the album's adventurous spirit is really articulated here, and Hillman's bass line is engaging.

The single reached 36 in the US, and the band's co-manager Eddie Tickner drummed-up publicity by claiming he'd taken out a £1,000,000 insurance policy against the band being abducted by aliens, in case this country music took a detour to outer space. However, McGuinn later conceded that the aliens wouldn't have heard it, because AM airwaves diffuse too quickly in space! Predictably po-faced, manager Jim Dickson felt the humour was misplaced. Though McGuinn might've naively thought the aliens might contact him if they heard him singing (it *was* 1966), a more poignant footnote is that the song has since been used to wake up astronauts on space shuttle expeditions!

'I See You' (Crosby, McGuinn)

This chestnut has a continuous euphoric chorus with a (what had by now become ubiquitous) McGuinn raga guitar break. Though McGuinn co-wrote the lyric, this was ostensibly a Crosby song. He was growing in confidence as a writer, was looking to push the boundaries with more-complex vocal harmonies, and helped move the band from songs dealing with Gene Clark's dark romanticism into psychological dramas about states of mind. This track reflects just how innovative the band were becoming.

Given its resemblance to John Coltrane's 'Impressions', it might've been written on the band's Dick Clark package tour when all they listened to was free jazz and Indian raga on the tour bus. Also influenced by the sambas of Coltrane's *A Love Supreme*, it has unexpected time signatures, lively percussion and an up-tempo bossa nova feel. Also, Crosby played the staccato rhythm guitar that drove the song on a road to where psychedelic pop met jazz-inflected folk rock.

Like all the best Byrds tracks, it doesn't hang around too long – just in two and a half minutes, its effortless harmonies and vigorous melody are offset by Crosby's amphetamine-driven jazz vamp, Clarke's rampaging drumming and McGuinn's thrilling, trippy and nervy guitar lilt. With its jazz-like raga-rock 12-string guitar runs and transformative harmonies, it was on the same astral plane as 'Eight Miles High'. The song's improvisational nature was highlighted by the stretched-out version on Yes' debut album, which suited Bill Bruford's jazz drumming. There's also a slightly longer Byrds' version on *Another Dimension,* with no overdubs and a more-audible arpeggio guitar part in the background.

With its airy folk-meets-bristly psychedelic guitar feel, it also influenced Love's *Forever Changes* more than a year later: especially 'Clarke & Hilldale'. Crosby continued with this vocal direction over the next few years.

'What's Happening?!?!' (Crosby)

This stark and unusual mid-tempo ballad was Crosby's first solo composition on a Byrds LP. It also featured piercing McGuinn guitar work with backwards guitar runs. McGuinn's stinging 12-string answers each Crosby vocal statement (philosophical questions about the changing times they were living in, man!) in a call-and-response effect. Crosby felt McGuinn's snaky guitar leads echoed what the lyric was asking. An added guitar drone continued the sound of 'Why' (see Connected Flights below), and was the first of Crosby's agnostic reflections on what life was all about, without getting close to anything like a resolution.

In retrospect, the lyric seems dated and asinine; all proto-hippie philosophising, questioning our place in the world. But it does showcase a band trying to push the envelope. McGuinn's psychedelic raga-rock break was realised by wiring his amp through small car speakers.

'I Come and Stand at Every Door' (Hikmet)

Like the first two albums, this one also includes a Pete Seeger adaptation. This Hiroshima-inspired folk song written by Turkish dissident Nazim Hikmet (who spent time in captivity) is the bleakest and most macabre song The Byrds ever recorded. The lyric is told from the perspective of the spirit of a seven-year-old Japanese child burned to death by radiation fallout following the horrors of the Hiroshima bombing. The melody is based on the traditional ballad 'Great Selchie of Shule Skerry', which McGuinn knew from Judy Collins' second album *Golden Apples of the Sun.* Michael Clarke provides a desolate marching rhythm, and like the last lines of 'Turn! Turn! Turn!', the song climaxes with Crosby's harmony, used to raise a more pragmatic peace message.

At the time, this probably appeared as socially conscious and quite edgy with its hypnotic chime/drone arrangement, but it now sounds ploddy and dated, and illustrates how much band politics were behind track selection. In retrospect, this could've been omitted and replaced by 'Psychodrama City' or 'I Know My Rider'. It's not the easiest listen, and it's a bit of a dour side closer. But then, most closing tracks are going to pale compared to side two's opener: a track where, again, they helped transform pop music.

'Eight Miles High' (McGuinn, Crosby, Clark)

The interchangeable terms psychedelic rock and acid rock were initially known as raga rock, as perhaps the single most-profound step towards the psychedelic world – and the most startling reflection of the Indian influence – was the astounding 'Eight Miles High'. It's distinguished by alluding to both jazz and raga music through channelling John Coltrane's 'India' and the Indian classical music of Ravi Shankar.

Originally cut at RCA Studios in late-1965, the song developed in stages, though McGuinn has always claimed it's fundamentally a folk song. Gene Clark devised the song's skeletal structure in a Pennsylvania hotel room while hanging out with The Rolling Stones' Brian Jones. The 1965 UK trip inspired Clark to pour the experience into a song with references to London streets, and McGuinn and Crosby added lines later. The song began as 'Six Miles High', but was changed to 'Eight' as it was more poetic and in line with The Beatles' 'Eight Days a Week'.

The sound was born out of the band listening to a cassette where one side had the music of John Coltrane, and the other side had the raga of Ravi Shankar. When Clark took the song to the band, they were already keen to emulate the music they'd been listening to. Indian culture and Crosby's jazz-inspired harmonies were a perfect match for the mysterious subject matter. Chris Hillman then introduced one of rock's great intros – a defining fanfare with a rumbling bass line, based on John Coltrane's intro to 'A Love Supreme'. The final piece of the jigsaw was McGuinn's extraordinary 12-string guitar runs, which – like 'Mr. Tambourine Man' – the song's feel was built around. McGuinn wanted the guitar to sound like a sax solo, and as the source of the four-note intro motif, he borrowed the most recognisable phrase from 'India' – Coltrane's 1961 experiment in Afro-Indian improvisation – and repeated it on the 12-string. 'Eight Miles High' was evidently part of a musical fusion sequence, as on 'India', Coltrane had himself alluded to ethnic music by borrowing a melody from a Vedic chant. McGuinn arranged the track with three raga solos, and by mirroring the sound of tenor saxophone valves opening and closing, he was looking for the sustain that Coltrane got from his instrument. The jagged modality made McGuinn's 12-string sound like a saxophone. Rod Argent's organ break (which was all over the place, knowing he could get away with a jazz break in a rock song) on The Zombies' 'She's Not There' was also an inspiration.

Clark had the chord structure and loose melody around which McGuinn transformed the new sound to a 12-string guitar, lending the song its constant coherence in a countermelody against ghostly, dronelike harmonies. Hillman and Clarke played brilliantly. Clarke's speedy snare fills were never better, playing fast and loose with the rhythm, and Hillman's bass complements the rattling cymbals perfectly. The Byrds were never more unified, and with some of the most avant-garde solos ever to make the charts, it's basically a frantic free-form freak-out. This was a completely new concept for pop music, where the end was like a raga metaphor for a plane coming in to land. Once it landed, those on board realised they'd been where they'd never been before. The Byrds were playing a kind of music that didn't even have a name yet!

Ultimately, this track dominates the album, and the result is psychedelia's first decisive declaration. The unique floating rhythms signalled an astonishing shift in the band's creative evolution. Twelve months earlier, they'd been just another bunch of struggling wannabes. Now, they'd shifted Coltrane's free-form runs onto a precedent-setting 12-string Rickenbacker raga symphony. The finished recording – perhaps The Byrds' greatest – was an aural representation of an LSD trip, and the ragas and modal-jazz nods were new, startling and irresistible. It was transcendental in that it elevated pop music to art and plunged the band into the new psychedelic maelstrom. Allied to Clark's gliding melody, this is where jazz and rock burst into psychedelic heaven. With its famous four-note riff and cascading harmonies, they were one of the first bands to take psychedelia into the mainstream. Achieving it by experimenting with different music forms, they didn't expect the psychedelic label – McGuinn had just been shooting for jazz. For him, it was more like early jazz fusion.

Time has shown the track to be one of the most extraordinary works in an extraordinary time, and briefly elevated the band to the creative level of The Beatles, who were encouraged by the possibilities of striking a balance between commercial boundaries and following their own muse. Indeed, early takes of *Revolver's* 'And Your Bird Can Sing' were deemed so Byrdsian that they had to change the arrangement.

With 'Eight Miles High' lines like 'Nowhere is there warmth to be found/ Among those afraid of losing their ground' suggesting a fragile, unsettled band of brothers, the words started to be analysed for other reasons. Though McGuinn has repeatedly maintained the word 'high' referred to air travel, Crosby unsurprisingly made links to its drug references. Possibly both stories regarding the lyric are correct. Clark's lines did refer to the UK trip, but Crosby's influence will certainly be drug-related. The title is perfect for either scenario.

But fate intervened, and the single's airplay and sales were affected. *The Gavin Report* was a radio-industry trade publication that top 40 programmers used to decide the content of programs, based on the report's tip sheets about possible inappropriate lyrics. With US vice president Spiro Agnew wading in by announcing that 'Eight Miles High' was a drug song, the BBC and American radio stations were in no doubt, and the song was banned. But the single's chart placing wasn't affected much. Suggestions it was banned a few weeks after release – meaning it stalled outside the top 10 due to lack of airplay – are simply not true. It was already going down the chart, and the relatively poor chart showings of 14 in the US and 24 in the UK weren't just down to reduced airplay. In truth, The Byrds were no longer a *pop* band, and the main reason the single missed the top 10 was for being too esoteric and progressive for early-1966 ears – after all, drug references didn't stop Dylan's 'Rainy Day Women #12 &35' reaching 2 in the US. Were large numbers of record buyers ready for this level of experimentation in early-1966? This was still nine months before 'Good Vibrations' was to hit number 1. In essence, it meant that The Byrds were no longer challengers to The Beatles – in terms of record sales anyway – and it basically ended The Byrds' career as a major singles band. They'd lost Middle America for good.

The initial critical reception was positive, with many welcoming the daring venture off the beaten track. *Record World* claimed it was an eerie tune with lyrics bound to hypnotise. But it was its influence on other musicians that was more immediate. To musicians like The Beatles, Bob Dylan (briefly) and burgeoning San Francisco bands like Jefferson Airplane and Grateful Dead, the psychedelic experience represented being open to possibility. With L.A. regarded as the land of dreams, San Francisco was seen as an esoteric hub, embracing left-field musical ideas, and by late-1966, the Haight Ashbury scene was an influential and creative community hub of Western pop culture. 'Eight Miles High' pointed the way forward. With its raga-rock drone of permanent harmonies and sitar-like guitar solos, it's where restless psychedelic eclecticism was born. Within weeks, Eastern-influenced tracks like The Yardbirds' 'Shapes of Things' and The Rolling Stones' 'Paint It Black' were heard on the radio, and longer improvisations – like The Paul Butterfield Blues Band's psych-blues-raga 'East West' were to be created.

Crosby preferred the RCA version, which he felt had more of a live, spontaneous feel and a more instinctive flow. (You can hear it on the album's CD reissue). The playing on the RCA version certainly has a natural live feel, but the gothic vocals on the released version are much smoother. Also worth checking out is the instrumental version on *Another Dimension*, where Crosby's shuddering rhythm guitar holds things together.

Today, 'Eight Miles High' sounds as timeless and daring as it did in 1966. That's probably because it avoids merely being guitar noodling. It was more about using the instrument to channel new sounds. Hillman still thinks it sounds truly creative, and poignantly thinks it's interesting to think where the band could've gone had they all stayed together, taking 'Eight Miles High' as a launching point. They wouldn't have necessarily ended up at *Sweetheart of the Rodeo* either! 'Eight Miles High' is still a lot of musicians' favourite Byrds track, and it's also McGuinn's favourite, feeling it was the band at their peak with its mid-1960s, random self-expression.

'Hey Joe (Where You Gonna Go)' (Roberts)

The Byrds' recording of this song is misjudged, and it's baffling why they never attempted a better version. Crosby introduced the band to the song, which he learned two years earlier from Dino Valente. After buying the rights from Billy Roberts, Valente claimed copyright under the pseudonym Chester Powers. But in light of all the garage-band covers at the time, Roberts negotiated a deal to get his publishing back.

The song was initially 'borrowed' from Niela Miller's 'Baby, Please Don't Go To Town'. When Miller and Roberts broke up, he kept the melody but changed the lyric.

Crosby was possessive about it, and got angry when Love and The Leaves released their versions. So, The Byrds relented and recorded their version with Crosby on lead vocal. The song epitomises the proto-punk L.A. garage sound more than any other from 1966, but not this version. While Crosby's phrasing is good, The Byrds' faster, lazy arrangement doesn't work, and he later admitted it was a mistake. It lacks any of their trademark harmony dynamics, and there's no ringing McGuinn solo to save the day this time. Their take has no real riff or prominent bass line, and the garage-band treatment doesn't hide an uninspired take. It's difficult to justify this take being included at the expense of much better ones. If they'd really cared for the song, they could've taken it to a similar place as the Shadows of Knight version, which was a longer and more-improvisational raga take.

The irony with the Byrds version is that Crosby arranged it as a rock-'n'-roll song. Many people learned it from Crosby, but most recorded superior versions – especially Jimi Hendrix's late-1966 one.

'Captain Soul' (Hillman, Crosby, Clarke, McGuinn)

This dopey R&B chug was recorded as a nod to Clarke's love of soul music. The rather obvious melody now sounds a bit hokey, and the track seems like nondescript filler. It was based on the riff to Lee Dorsey's 'Get Out of My Life Woman' and was originally (unimaginatively) titled 'Three Minute Break' until Hillman came up with 'Captain Soul'.

Michael Clarke thought he deserved more of the publishing, and later labelled the other writers as 'cruel bastards', thinking the four-way writing credit was unfair considering his contribution. He also provided the breathy harmonica break, which at least added something different. It's a catchy enough instrumental, with Hillman's funky bass almost acting as the lead instrument, and McGuinn always thought it was interesting. Oddly, as part of a play on this song, a Texan garage band called The Livin' End wrote a song called 'Captain's Soul' which has the same Lee Dorsey riff with added vocals. You can find it on YouTube.

As an interesting footnote – of all the 1966 Byrds recordings, Gene Clark only appears on the 'Eight Miles High'/'Why' single and this. But the fact he has no writing credit suggests he had very little input here.

'John Riley' (Gibson, Neff; Arr. McGuinn, Hillman, Clarke, Crosby)
Still alluding to folk traditions, this is a perfect example of a transition piece
at this early career stage. The group now arranged these standards with their
ethereal backing vocals and layers of experimental instrumentation. It's the
sound of The Byrds doing traditional folk in a new way.

Also known as 'A Fair Young Maid All in Her Garden', the song was derived
from Homer's *Odyssey,* and adapted through the English folk-ballad tradition.
A done-to-death staple of the then-recent folk revival, the band completely
reinvented it, using McGuinn's swivelling 12-strings and classic Byrds
harmonies. It illustrates their ability to make ancient tales seem contemporary
– encapsulated here with the arrangement laminated in gorgeous strings,
creating a dramatic feel.

Like their interpretation of 'Wild Mountain Thyme', the rich folk
orchestration illustrated The Byrds' developing musical maturity. McGuinn
was always beguiled by the Joan Baez version – especially her delicate
fingerpicking, and both Baez and The Byrds based their versions on Bob
Gibson's late-1950s interpretation. Paradoxically, while the strings and guitars
add grace and majesty to The Byrds' version, Clarke's drums add authority.
With crashing cymbals, it's where drone-like guitars merge with folk,
delivering a perfect transformative interpretation.

The CD reissue includes a tantalising instrumental take with a much faster
tempo and raga lilt. It positively swings, and the differences make some parts
almost unrecognisable. There's also a version on *Another Dimension* with no
string overdubs: interesting to hear, but it's better with the orchestration.

R.E.M.'s Peter Buck always loved the chord changes on this track, and
claimed it influenced his guitar-playing.

'2-4-2 Fox Trot (The Lear Jet Song)' (McGuinn)
Continuing the tradition of quirky album closers, this was actually a McGuinn
original. Even though it's full of studio trickery, it's catchy enough, with a decent
chorus (though it does become too repetitive) and some propulsive Clarke
drumming. McGuinn and Crosby liked the song, seeing it as an extension of their
sound-effect experimentation. McGuinn has always denied that the jet sound of
the track was a vacuum cleaner – he's adamant it was a Lear jet. Moreover, by
now, he was friends with Bill Lear's pilot son, who took the group on a flight
with Peter Fonda, and the 2-4-2 came from John Lear's personal jet registration.
They felt particularly vindicated when The Beatles used similar effects on 'Yellow
Submarine'. On *Another Dimension*, there's a version without the sound effects.

The track was primarily an excuse to indulge McGuinn's obsession with
maths, science and aeronautics. In 1965, an *NME* journalist asked McGuinn
why he had a slide rule in his jacket pocket, and he cryptically replied that he
always carried it, 'Just in case'.

The track might've been influential in its use of electronic effects, but it's
slender – or is everything being unfairly compared to 'Eight Miles High' now?

Connected Flights
'Why' (McGuinn, Crosby)

Crosby became entranced with Indian ragas after sitting in on a Ravi Shankar recording session in 1964. This homage to his growing raga fascination was launched by McGuinn's sitar-like drone, and is a beacon of psychedelic raga rock.

It was recorded in December 1965 while the folk-rock 'Turn! Turn! Turn!' was still at number one in *Billboard*, but they were way ahead of the curve, and the song eventually graced the 'Eight Miles High' B-side. It's a *tour de force* from the days when bands made great B-sides and not always just throwaways for publishing reasons. McGuinn's sustained Rickenbacker sounds tremendous, considering it's played through a walkie-talkie inside a cigar box, and Crosby's vocals are more ornate than those on other versions of the song. This track probably inspired the term raga rock more than any other, as it drew more directly on Indian raga, though the clanging chord at the end briefly returns them to their folk-rock roots. Crosby's sturdy rhythm guitar, Hillman's loping bass run and McGuinn's drone created the perfect blend, made glorious by the scorching sitar-like solo at the end. It sounds so *way out*, but it's not a sitar. The Byrds *never* used a sitar on any record. Though they attended a 1966 press conference with a sitar, they were merely posturing.

Crosby always claimed McGuinn added nothing to this composition and shouldn't have gotten a co-writing credit. But in addition to the raga guitar breaks, McGuinn *did* suggest changing the line 'You keep saying no to me' to 'You keep saying no to her'. For all its Eastern sound – which clearly influenced the Velvet Underground's 'White Light White Heat' – the verses are Motown-like, and when Crosby counts in verse three with 'Ooohhh', it's sublime.

Like the A-side, a previous version had been recorded at RCA, which they had to re-record for legal reasons. Both versions are much better versions than the one on 1967's almost-immaculate *Younger Than Yesterday* album: more of which later.

'I Know My Rider (I Know You Rider)' (Arr. McGuinn, Clark, Crosby)

Usually titled 'I Know You Rider', Crosby actually recorded a version of this before the 1964 Jet Set demos. Two years on, the Byrds version was directly influenced by the feel of The Beatles' 'Paperback Writer', with McGuinn aiming for an acid-tinged sitar sound on his guitar, which gloriously twists its way around the song. As such, The Byrds' version is best known for its nod to Ravi Shankar, especially on the instrumental break. If you listen closely, you can hear McGuinn simultaneously sing the last phrase of each guitar solo. This vocal part was an overdub on the original multitrack, and producer Stanton used it as sweetening. Also, Clarke's drum rolls are effortless on this version.

Although the band didn't enjoy recording this due to the amount of takes, McGuinn suspects the reason this track was never released originally was just down to politics. This is probably true, as they recorded the song three times, and this version could've easily graced the album, especially helping to bolster side two. At one point, the track was rumoured to be their next single, and was a much-more-commercial proposition than its intended predecessor, '5D'.

This track also appears in the *Cancelled Flights* box set.

'Psychodrama City' (Crosby)

This was planned for but cut from the album, and first released on the *Never Before* compilation. Again, this showcases Crosby's confidence in working with weird, free-flowing musings based on spectral jazz structures and there's a Mose Allison feel to the vocal. Its inclusion – at the expense of 'Captain Soul' or 'Hey Joe' – would've made the album even stronger and it would've sat nicely after 'Eight Miles High' as a sort-of comedown from the highs of that side-two opener.

After the bluesy improvised intro, it enters the new world of acid-drenched Crosby vocals and improvised McGuinn guitar innovations, punctuated by his raga-tinged Rickenbacker work. Crosby's vocals were overdubbed later, and his lyric – which referenced modern L.A. and Gene Clark's departure – predated the early-1970s singer-songwriter scene. The track was mooted as a possible B-side to 'I Know My Rider', though it never materialised. It was worthy of being worked on more in 1966, though. But this version is more than decent, and appears in the *Cancelled Flights* box set.

Also – for Byrd maniacs – the 1990 box set version has a slightly longer guitar intro than the *Never Before* version, and an instrumental version on *Another Dimension* has extra rhythm guitar and raga runs throughout.

Afterword

It's a really innovative, if uneven, album dominated by side two's futuristic jigsaw opener. It's astonishing to think that 'Eight Miles High' was recorded only seven weeks after the rather twee folk standard 'He Was a Friend Of Mine'. But this was the mid-1960s when things moved so incredibly fast.

The Byrds' audience had diminished, and the band were now experimenting with different styles and becoming more esoteric. Chris Hillman was writing more, and the band were forging ahead of most of their rivals. Taking their magic carpet to new heights, they were to explore new musical tracts, and their best work was yet to come.

Younger Than Yesterday (1967)

Personnel:
Jim McGuinn: 12 string guitar, vocals
David Crosby: rhythm guitar, vocals
Chris Hillman: bass, vocals
Michael Clarke: drums
Hugh Masekela: horns
Vern Gosdin: acoustic guitar
Clarence White: electric guitar
Producer: Gary Usher
Record label: Columbia, CBS (UK)
Release date: 6 February 1967
Chart position: UK: 37, US: 24
Running time: 29:11

The band recorded their fourth album *Younger Than Yesterday,* in 11 days in December 1966; released just two months later. Permanently gone was the star of mid-tempo melancholy ballads, but the album built further on the eclecticism of *Fifth Dimension* and pushed The Byrds into more kaleidoscopic areas.

Gary Usher produced the album, and it's no coincidence that this coincided with the group's most creative phase. Usher gave each album project an overview. For a short time, he was essentially The Byrds' spark plug: their George Martin. Usher was most famous for co-writing The Beach Boys' 'In My Room' with Brian Wilson, but he fell out with Wilson's domineering father, Murry, and – as Usher was known for being a studio innovator – The Byrds grabbed the chance to work with him. He proved to be The Byrds' most invaluable producer; able to match their glorious sonic visions.

The album was an artistic triumph, propelling the group further into the underground scene. It was more varied than previous albums, and, guided by Usher's studio trickery, the group moved effortlessly between genres, mixing psychedelia with folk rock and country. The former folk rockers were now truly harbingers of psychedelia with a futuristic bent. In fact, they were even christened the innovators of space rock, due to some of the subject matter. The album was a West Coast *Revolver* – while the previous album had merged Coltrane and Shankar, this one combined Stockhausen, bluegrass and African rhythms.

Meanwhile, though McGuinn and Crosby shared a far-out curiosity, their relationship was becoming increasingly fractious. While Crosby felt a constant struggle to get his songs recorded, he was taking his writing to new levels and trying to adopt a more prominent role in the band. He had a great way of finding interesting progressions. He was also having a huge influence on the burgeoning counterculture.

Hillman was becoming a confident bass player, incorporating lots of leads. But it was his emergence as a strong composer that was a huge sea change for the band at this time, as they now had three songwriters and weren't as dependant on covers or Gene Clark's ballads. (Apparently, Clark broke down when he first heard *Younger Than Yesterday*, aware of how creatively far behind his old bandmates he was.) Hillman was quietly becoming the group's most prolific songwriter, and wrote half the album. His songs not only raised his stakes as an increasingly original writer but pointed the band in their next direction, incorporating an increasing bluegrass influence.

The new album followed on from 'Mr Spaceman' by recording rock music with a country tinge, long before cosmic cowboy Gram Parsons joined the band. Bluegrass guitarist and ex-Kentucky Colonel Clarence White appeared as a session musician: a prologue to a later chapter. His main influence was James Burton – the king of rock-'n'-roll session guitarists – whom White always felt was the first to do the 'country thing' on the guitar.

Continuing their trend of not standing still, the group added an experimental feel with more electric instruments, and trumpet player Hugh Masekela appeared on 'So You Want to Be a Rock 'n' Roll Star'. He became the first African musician to perform with a Western rock band when he appeared with The Byrds at the Monterey Pop Festival in June 1967.

Their increasing creativity continued to co-exist with those intensifying rivalries. While band politics festered, they even considered cutting a final album (*Sanctuary*) and starting solo careers. Crosby was now hanging out with Buffalo Springfield, and Stephen Stills regularly challenged McGuinn to play like him, and McGuinn assumed Crosby was baiting him through Stills. At Monterey, Crosby ranted, trashed the Warren Commission report on JFK's assassination, and advocated the benefits of LSD, which heightened tensions.

Though reviews were good, the album was not as popular with the band's decreasing teen audience, and the record found a niche with the new underground scene: seen as the natural format for an idiom pushing its commercial and creative limits. Critics were full of praise for the innovative, forward-thinking music. And though there was nothing as groundbreaking as 'Eight Miles High', respect for the album as a cohesive artistic statement was universal. *Melody Maker* said it surpassed all the group's other works, being rich in sparkling ideas, and added that if you ignored this album, you were not only foolish but deaf! *Mojo Navigator* labelled it a modern symphony.

The cover art – probably the band's greatest – has the spirits of the new Byrds leaving their old bodies. Man! One question, though: who are all the young faces on the back cover? I've never quite worked that out!

It's one of The Byrds' most ambitious and wide-ranging albums, featuring some of their most majestic work. Arriving only seven months after *Fifth Dimension,* it was the first Byrds album with Gary Usher as producer and is a meeting of minds (that would be fully realised on the masterful follow-up). It simultaneously exists in the pop mainstream, with nods to folk and early psychedelia, while pointing towards a more-inventive and hazy acid-folk pop with an increasing nod to country rock.

By merging charming melodies and experimentation, The Byrds were now Southern California cool personified; cerebral rather than sentimental. It's a near-perfect collection.

'So You Want to Be a Rock 'n' Roll Star' (McGuinn, Hillman)

The Byrds do satire! After returning from a Letta Mbule session, including South African trumpeter Hugh Masekela who The Byrds met on tour, Hillman had an insistent riff swirling around his head, and it soon became the beginning of the most celebrated McGuinn/Hillman collaboration. Trading lines and ideas in rapid-fire fashion (most of it was written overlooking Laurel Canyon), the duo completed the surprisingly commercial song in about 40 minutes, with McGuinn basing his guitar motif on a lick he heard from Miriam Makeba guitarist Miller Thomson.

The lyric was inspired by publicist Derek Taylor who suggested they use their frustration with the growing number of manufactured pop groups to write a satirical song about the *ingredients* needed to be a pop star. While the lyric was a comment on the process bands like The Monkees, it wasn't a dig at them individually, as Peter Tork was actually a friend and neighbour. It was more about the phenomena of one-hit wonders, and the commentary – however perceptive – was meant to be satire, not sour grapes. Considering Michael Clarke was recruited because he looked like Brian Jones, maybe there was also a hint of self-parody involved.

The song also had a slightly prophetic autobiographical element, being an ironic comment on the group's roller coaster over the last two years. They were now experiencing the strange game of the final verse's acceptance of fading stardom. The irony wasn't lost when Derek Taylor suggested merging audience screams from 1965 Byrds shows into Hillman's riff, as the days of crazy teens screaming at Byrds concerts were now gone.

In addition to the obligatory McGuinn guitar solo, there's also a trumpet solo from Hugh Masekela. It starts the album floating in the ether: a band playing at their fluid best. The trebly sound complements the hard-driving, pulsating guitar line and those penetrating trumpet lines.

The single's January-1967 release returned The Byrds to the US top 30, though it failed to chart in the UK. But in the intervening years, 'So You Want to Be a Rock 'n' Roll Star' has become one of their best-known songs, and is now accorded classic status. Following on from a contemporary cover by The Move, it even entered the lexicon of punk when The Patti Smith Group covered it. There have also been numerous live versions, including those by R.E.M. and Pearl Jam.

The single is now seen as the band's farewell to pop, and – ironically – by the time it started falling down the charts, *More of The Monkees* reached number one in the album charts! Writer Dave Marsh commented that ironically the music makes the song so enticing, that it has probably spawned more bands than it's discouraged. He's right, and the song is still alluring today.

'Have You Seen Her Face' (Hillman)

This is Hillman's first solo credit, and he wrote more songs on this album than McGuinn or Crosby. The inspiration for the song came after Hillman attended recording sessions for 'So You Want to Be a Rock 'N Roll Star', and he wrote it when working with Hugh Masekela and other South African musicians. But the single was a flop in the USA, and wasn't released in the UK.

Hillman's emergence as a canny songwriter, offset Crosby's jazz/psychedelic experiments and McGuinn's increasing obsession with studio trickery, to help develop the Byrds' creative gumbo. Here, his understated Harrison-singing-a-McCartney-song vocal style is a subtle counterpoint to his melodic Beatlesque bass lines. The song is like Merseybeat shot-through with the new hip Los Angeles scene. With its choppy rhythm (there's even some honky tonk piano), there's such an energy, and it's like an early version of Britpop melodicism.

McGuinn used Crosby's Gretsch guitar for the elevated, ringing six-string solo, creating a more-groovy model of the 'Eight Miles High' free raga. Crosby's harmonies are so well-crafted that they enhance the track as much as McGuinn's guitar runs, and Hillman particularly admired the way Crosby came in and out of the lead vocal.

Byrdfact: the version on the 1990 box set has a longer ending.

'C.T.A.-102' (McGuinn, Hippard)

A sibling of 'Mr. Spaceman', this whimsical psychedelic piece indulged McGuinn's space-cowboy fixation and included alien-like voice effects. It was an example of McGuinn absorbing and realising new ideas in the studio.

Though the song sounds a bit dated now, it does make sense in the context of what bands were doing (and taking) in 1967. For all its Stockhausen experimentation, it has a bluegrass-influenced folk-rock structure – especially the middle instrumental passage (where it would've been nice if the guitar was louder). Co-written by McGuinn's friend Robert Hippard, it was labelled space rock at the time due to its astronomical subject matter. McGuinn considered contacting celestial bodies, initially unaware that stars disintegrate at tremendous speeds. (Ever the experimenter, he continued the space-rock theme on the next album, with 'Space Odyssey'.)

McGuinn and Usher playfully reversed the sped-up speaking voice at the end so fans would play the record backwards, but it was just nonsense being spoken. Considerable time was spent in finding sound effects in an age when synthesizers were still to be utilised. The Stockhausen-like experiment – where they used an oscillator with a telegraph key, with the audible bang created by fists on the console while the piano sustain pedal was held down – was the kind of thing simultaneously happening in the Abbey Road studios.

A far-out footnote is that at the end of the song, the aliens are supposed to be listening back to the track and replying. McGuinn took great pride in the song being mentioned in an astrophysics magazine.

'Renaissance Fair' (Crosby, McGuinn)

Hillman's loping bass playing was also blossoming and adding new texture. This harmony-soaked dynamic track was basically a Crosby song, and was about an early flower-child gathering. Crosby's smooth arpeggio has an otherworldly feel. It still sounds like a medieval fair: albeit a chemically-enhanced one. Though McGuinn and Crosby had a fire-and-ice relationship, it had little effect on the music, and probably encouraged them to outdo each other creatively. In the studio, creative ideas and arrangements with psychedelic majesty soared under the guidance of Gary Usher. At one stage, this song was going to have a jazz lilt, but the soprano sax was removed from the final mix.

Instead of writing a paean about the fair itself, Crosby used the senses to describe the serene feelings. The twisting guitar intro gives way to the counter-harmonies floating around the slipstream, while the lyric adds colour to the benign psychedelic scenery.

Eric Burdon based his song 'Monterey' on 'Renaissance Fair' and used the 'I think that maybe I'm dreaming' line when performing it at the Monterey Pop Festival, in June 1967. Stephen Stills' marvellous Buffalo Springfield song 'Rock & Roll Woman' was based on the 'Renaissance Fair' melody too.

Byrd trivia: This was the first song The Byrds played on the Monterey Festival stage that summer; a stage partly built by a young carpenter called Harrison Ford. He also later built a kitchen for the McGuinns' Laurel Canyon home!

'Time Between' (Hillman)

Though he was never a fan of the term country rock, Hillman told *Uncut* magazine in 2003: 'That's a country song, if not the first country-rock song!'. It was the first song he ever wrote – even more impressive considering the infectious melody. The short track packs a punch and predates The Byrds' later country-rock exploration with a sweeping chorus, replete with great harmonies. It sounds like countrified British Invasion pop.

Hillman's bluegrass background was starting to influence The Byrds' sound, and essentially the track has a bluegrass rhythm with a backbeat. The song also includes an unsurpassable guitar break from session musician and future Byrd Clarence White – foreshadowing the group's future output, and helping herald the term 'Americana'. Hillman hired White to give the guitar break a country feel, and felt that though White didn't play a lot of notes, those he *did* play were very moving. Hillman's old friend Vern Gosdin played acoustic guitar and sang a harmony part, though Crosby got annoyed and replaced the harmony with his own, even though Hillman thought Gosdin's was slightly better. Hillman has called this period the 'descent into hell', referring to the band's fractious relationship with Crosby. But it certainly didn't hamper Hillman's emerging songwriting talent. His love of longer lines and his ease with an infectious melody were blossoming. The lyric referred to his burgeoning relationship with Kit Lambert's secretary Anya Buter, who Hillman later married.

My only criticism of this track is that it should be longer, where White could have stretched out more with the sort of guitar break he played when performing the song live in future years.

'Everybody's Been Burned' (Crosby)

The B-side of 'So You Want Be a Rock 'n' Roll Star' was a *new* Crosby song. Up to this point, he'd mostly sufficed with co-writes, but with the departure of Gene Clark, Crosby and Hillman upped their songwriting game. In fact, by late-1966, both surpassed McGuinn as the band's main songwriters. This was clearly Crosby's greatest song to this point, but unlike Hillman, Crosby had been writing for a few years, and this jazz-scented rumination on a failed love affair, written before he met the band, was originally conceived as a folk-club torch ballad.

Though structurally less ambitious than newer Crosby songs, this bossa-nova-influenced track almost dwarfed everything else on the album. The E-minor drone foresaw the chords and melodies Crosby would use on future recordings: especially on his debut solo album. The contemplative lyric describes a relationship straddling disappointment and resolution. It's one of Crosby's most heartbreaking songs, sung with a tact at odds with his impulsive nature.

With a laid-back jazz groove, Crosby's sensitive vocal style, Hillman's jazz bass runs and one of McGuinn's most glorious and glistening solos (moving between eastern raga and jazz), it was a testament to the band's growing audacity. Also – for Byrdmaniacs – the shaker heard in the stereo mix is not on the mono version! But generally speaking, the mono mixes of early Byrds albums are better, if you're interested in that sort of thing.

Oddly, Crosby never wanted to record this song for their debut album or even perform it live. The CD re-release of *Preflyte Sessions* included an unheard early version of the song, alongside other pre-Byrd Crosby demos.

A song about hopelessness has never sounded so gorgeous. This haunting and divinely melancholy track is one of The Byrds' greatest songs.

'Thoughts and Words' (Hillman)

This is perhaps *the* hidden Byrds chestnut, and strangely it barely appears on compilations. By now, they were effortlessly hip at creating a sensitive form of rock that didn't have to be macho, and this elegant Hillman song is one of his finest.

But he wasn't shy to credit McGuinn and producer Gary Usher for their arrangement input. The track encapsulates the 1966/1967 Byrds perfectly – dynamic studio experimentation with a constant desire to sound different from before. With its ascending chords, pulsing bass and sitar-like, shimmering backwards guitars, the track is decorated with Crosby's gorgeous drone-like vocal counterpoint. This melting pot blends a *Rubber Soul*-type pop and an LSD-laden folk-rock contemplation.

With this sort of form, it makes you wonder if The Byrds would've survived Clark's departure without Hillman's emergence as a songwriter of great craft. The lyric is about the nature of the mind and human relationships, including betrayal. That tends to get lost in the majestic arrangement, which embodies the group's experimental spirit – illustrated best by those acid-soaked call-and-response harmonies on the closing verse.

'Mind Gardens' (Crosby)
The band's limitless free expression could lead to folly. This song title might suggest a philosophical and sophisticated lyric married to ethereal Eastern-tinged instrumentation, but nothing could be further from the truth. The conceit of the song – aiming for a melodramatic swagger – ultimately failed, and is the original lineup's creative nadir.

The song has no drum rhythm, and sounds especially silly on the Shakespeare quotes, which are hugely pretentious. If any slack could be cut, it's that they were constantly trying to push boundaries and create more complex structures. Crosby perfected these ideas in 1971 on his solo debut, but this track is an early example of his freak flag flying just a bit too high!

It works best where it audaciously tries to come in and out of raga, but the other band members didn't want it on the album. McGuinn said it had no rhythm, meter or rhyme. In addition to its tunelessness, McGuinn and Hillman also complained of Crosby's blaring vocal self-indulgence. The backwards guitars try to complement the druggy lyric surrealism, but it ends up sounding strangled. It crosses the line of invention, suggesting its author was too stoned or narcissistic to notice it was a bad song. But Crosby fought to include it on the album – a song dealing with how building walls around your mind to keep out pain can also shut out happiness (I think!).

Crosby later admitted that the song wasn't very good. It now sounds typical of some experimental late-1960s psychedelia and has dated badly. The alternate take on the CD reissue adds nothing but some slightly different vocal phrasing. There's an instrumental version at the end of the extra reissue track 'Old John Robertson', and it's probably more listenable without the vocals and backwards guitars.

The Byrds' raga dream faded here, as the sitar-like guitar sound was never used on any subsequent Byrds song. So, let's remember that sound for the joys of tracks like 'Eight Miles High' and 'Why', but not this!

'My Back Pages' (Dylan)
This is the first Byrds track I ever heard. Within 20 seconds, I was transfixed by the languid guitar and the surreal lyric imagery. After 30 seconds – when those Canyon harmonies kick in – I realised my musical life would never be

the same. The lines 'Ah, but I was so much older then/I'm younger than that now' are probably the greatest ever Byrds harmonies.

Estranged manager Jim Dickson suggested that the band record this Dylan song, originally on his pre-electric 1964 album *Another Side of Bob Dylan*. Here Dylan was starting to withdraw from his protest-singer role. He was talking about creative liberation, as he didn't want to preach anymore, since he felt that when you preach you become your own enemy.

This may be The Byrds' best Dylan cover. Dickson once referred to McGuinn as his only brush with genius, and you can hear it here. They essentially transform a plain Dylan dirge into a sparkling folk-rock gem by changing the meter from 3/4 to 4/4. Where Dylan sneered his lyric, McGuinn's vocal is emotive and sublime. As a listener, you truly believe that wisdom genuinely comes from experience whenever you hear McGuinn sing that chorus of winsome nostalgia. He also cooked up that classic opening guitar lick, and his breakout solo is dreamlike and perhaps his peak as a Byrd, especially those last chiming notes. It's such a natural reinvention, where their version has an innate grace and grandeur. They make the song their own; the voices lifting it to euphoric heights with added tenderness, that wonderful chorus evoking the hippie ethos more than any other song. There's also a lovely organ part, played by Cecil Barnard. Dylan has performed it live since 1988, and has used The Byrds version as a template – most memorably when a cast of special guests – including George Harrison, Neil Young and McGuinn – played alongside him in 1992 at his 30th-anniversary concert.

But Crosby felt recording another Dylan song was a bit of a cop-out, a backward step, and was formulaic in trying to brazenly recapture 'Mr. Tambourine Man'. Others also thought this might be a regression, but it became irrelevant when they heard it, and critics praised McGuinn for a memorable performance and a classic Rickenbacker solo.

An earlier version was recorded that was put through a Leslie cabinet speaker, and according to Gary Usher, it was mooted as a single (It appears on the *Cancelled Flights* box.) However, an edited version of the album cut was eventually released as a single and reached the US top 30, proving to be the band's last US top-40 hit. In a letter he wrote to Byrds management, Columbia Vice-President Clive Davis said it was classic Byrds, and felt they had a long future if they continued to work with folk-rock melodies. He said they had to achieve the tremendous potential they were capable of. But artistically – if not commercially – they were already doing that, and continued to do so throughout 1967 and 1968. It was still less than two years since 'Mr. Tambourine Man' had broken through, but so much creativity had been born in that short time.

A masterpiece distinguished by McGuinn's great Rickenbacker lines and those divine, reflective harmonies, the song gave the album its title, in a roundabout way. It also cemented the band's reputation as the definitive interpreters of Dylan's work.

'The Girl With No Name' (Hillman)
Clarence White features (uncredited) on this Hillman composition, and like 'Time Between', it's a straight folk/country track. With characteristic Byrds harmonies, White's bluegrass guitar fingerpicking imitates banjo lines.

It's another great offering and continued the writer's theme of failed relationships. But in hindsight, like 'Time Between' it should've been longer. Maybe with more songwriting experience and confidence, Hillman might've suggested a longer bluegrass break – a sound that was gradually entering the band's repertoire.

The lyric was not about a prostitute as had been assumed, but was about a failed love affair with a real girl: Girl Freiberg. Her real name was Julia Dreyer: referred to as Girl because she was the only daughter in a family of boys. She married David Freiberg of Quicksilver Messenger Service.

'Why' (McGuinn, Crosby)
This broke the tradition of joke endings, kind of. It was a strange end for the album. It was Crosby's idea to rework this, and the band flattered him by allowing another of his songs on the album. But if that's the case, why didn't they just use an outtake – like his 'It Happens Each Day' – instead of this restrained version of a recent glorious B-side? Irrespective of suitable alternatives being available, it was still an odd decision to end the album with an inferior version of a previously recorded song, especially since the definitive raga version recorded almost a year earlier was infinitely superior to this diluted copy. Though it's a great song, this version pales next to the driving force of the 'Eight Miles High' B-side or even the original RCA version. Though it's sonically clearer, the solo is flatter-sounding, and without McGuinn's spidery sitar-like guitar break (the highlight of both original versions), this version sounds quite tame.

Crosby later admitted that the RCA version was his favourite.

Connected Flights
'It Happens Each Day' (Crosby)
In one of his finest songs to this point, Crosby multitracked his mellow harmonies for the first time. Yet 'Mind Gardens' took this track's place on the album! (And the limp rework of 'Why'! – for all their friction, even Terry Melcher probably wouldn't have let this happen).

It has a cool, jazzlike feel and Crosby's soon-to-be-obligatory sea imagery. But it was deemed unfinished at the time, and for the 1987 *Never Before* project, Hillman and Jim Dickson added acoustic guitar to fill it out. Crosby admitted that after he heard the 1987 version, he regretted not making more use of acoustic guitar in his Byrds days, as he'd concentrated solely on electric.

This is included on the *Cancelled Flights* box set as the proposed B-side of the Leslie-speaker version of 'My Back Pages', and even without the acoustic guitar, this should've been on the album: especially side two.

'Don't Make Waves' (McGuinn, Hillman)

Considering this is an unadulterated, banal and risible pastiche, and includes Crosby's ironic and frankly, arrogant 'masterpiece' put-down at the end (It was a quick song made for a beach film after all), this is listenable enough. The version in the dreadful film of the same name has a different mix with added dopey harmonies near the end.

This is the single version (the 'Have You Seen Her Face' B-side) and clearly recalls McGuinn's Brill Building-era songs. The film version is better and has an obvious lysergic thing going on, although – unforgivably – McGuinn's solo is faded just as it gets going.

For completists, the mono mix of 'Don't Make Waves' made its first album appearance on the 1982 *The Original Singles: 1967-1969, Volume 2* compilation, and can also be found on the Sundazed compilation *The Columbia Singles '65-'67*. The stereo mix is a bonus track on the 1996 *Younger Than Yesterday* CD reissue. You can find the film version on YouTube.

At a little over 90 seconds in length, this is the shortest Byrds studio track.

'Roll Over Beethoven' (Live) (Berry)

From a Swedish radio broadcast in 1967, this is a rather tepid run-through of the Chuck Berry standard. The song was a staple of their live repertoire from 1965 to 1968, and this version appeared on the 1990 *The Byrds* box set. They performed this live into the 1970s, and a version appeared on *Straight For the Sun* from a 1971 college radio broadcast. There's also a version on the *Banjoman* soundtrack (along with a version of 'Mr. Tambourine Man') from the Clarence White-era Byrds, which also features John Guerin on drums. But generally, The Byrds don't really do rock 'n' roll very convincingly.

'Lady Friend' (Crosby)

Considering the group conflicts by the summer of 1967, it was incredible that Crosby got an A-side (the only Byrds single entirely written by him). However difficult Crosby was to work with, leaving this classic off the follow-up album was a denial that he ever existed. The song is discussed here because it appeared on the *Younger Than Yesterday* CD reissue, even though it was recorded after that album's release.

With its glorious reverb, this was a scorching single, and it's a tragedy it wasn't a massive hit. Considering it has the same euphoric feel as The Turtles' 'Happy Together' or one of those harmony-soaked Association tracks (like the bridge on 'Never My Love'), it should've been a Summer of Love hit, and is one of The Byrds' greatest singles. Even the press predicted the band would return to the higher end of the charts with this song. But by this time, perhaps the band was deemed too underground to get much airplay anymore.

This song, about the fragments of a broken relationship, is sublime. With its punchy rock production, the horns, in particular, preempt a lot of late-1960s psychedelic rock. While the brass parts have more momentum (Crosby

Above: The classic 1965 lineup, which pioneered the folk rock genre. (*Alamy*)

Left: *Mr Tambourine Man*. The debut album included Beatlised versions of Dylan songs, folk standards and some Gene Clark originals. (*Columbia*)

Right: *Turn! Turn! Turn!* The second album, and as with the debut, the title track was a US number-one single. (*Columbia*)

Right: *Fifth Dimension*. The first of the mid-1960s 'Holy Trinity' and the first to include their psychedelic logo. (*Columbia*)

Left: *Younger Than Yesterday*. The second of the 'Holy Trinity', where Chris Hillman started blossoming as a writer. (*Columbia*)

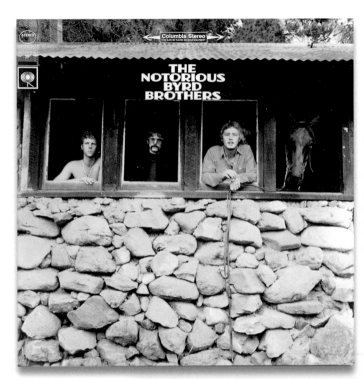

Left: *Notorious Byrd Brothers.* The last of the 'Holy Trinity' and their absolute masterpiece, with a gorgeous Gary Usher production. (*Columbia*)

Right: The country rock template: *Sweetheart of the Rodeo.* The album they made with the cosmic cowboy, Gram Parsons. (*Sony Legacy*)

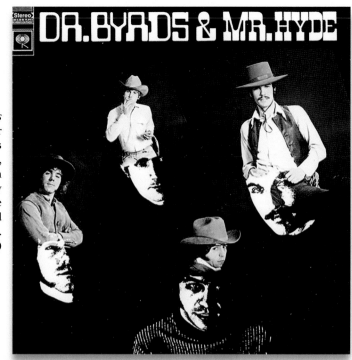

Right: *Dr Byrds & Mr Hyde*. Their pioneering days were behind them, but this album still had a new sound with some harder-edged blues numbers. (*Columbia*)

Left: *Ballad of Easy Rider*. This gentle, pastoral album was the last album to feature John York on bass. (*Columbia*)

Left: The Jet Set. Pictured during the early days when McGuinn, Clark and Crosby bonded over harmonies and The Beatles. (*Sundazed*)

Right: Pictured during the ill-fated 1965 UK tour. However, they hung out with The Beatles and expanded their material after this meeting. (*Chris Walter*)

Left: When they returned to the States, the band appeared on the Ed Sullivan Show. (*Columbia*)

Above: The original five piece: Crosby, McGuinn, Hillman, Clark and Clarke perfecting their cool and aloof image.

Left: The Byrds' sets at Ciro's helped the Sunset Strip become a major gathering place for the emerging counterculture. (*Getty Images*)

Right: After the main songwriter Gene left; David, Chris and Jim began pushing their own songwriting.

Left: *(Untitled).* The law of diminishing returns kicks in, but the album included 'Chestnut Mare', which returned them to the UK charts. (*Columbia*)

Right: *Byrdmaniax.* This album was their nadir. The death masks were a good metaphor for the music. (*Columbia*)

Right: *Farther Along.* The quickly recorded follow-up to the over-produced *Byrdmaniax* was another mediocre effort. (*Columbia*)

Left: *Byrds.* The ill-fated reunion album which re-united the original lineup. (*Asylum*)

Above: The Byrds' experiments in early psychedelia influenced the San Francisco scene, the creative hub where the new counter-culture was most evident. (*Getty Images*)

Below: McGuinn's classic 12-string Rickenbacker guitar: the sound of a new jingle jangle morning. (*gearformusic.com*)

Above: Clarence White's Stringbender, designed by bandmate Gene Parsons. (*United Musicians Radio*)

Below: The best live version of the Byrds and the most stable lineup: White, (Gene) Parsons, McGuinn and Battin.

THE BYRDS

ALL I REALLY WANT TO DO

 1947

Left: The 'All I Really Want To Do' UK single. It made the UK top five in 1965. (*Columbia/CBS*)

Right: 'Eight Miles High'. Perhaps their finest moment and the song that helped pioneer acid rock. (*Columbia*)

THE BYRDS
EIGHT MILES HIGH

mr. spaceman
LES BYRDS

Left: Byrd flights from around the world: the French 'Mr. Spaceman' single. (*Columbia*)

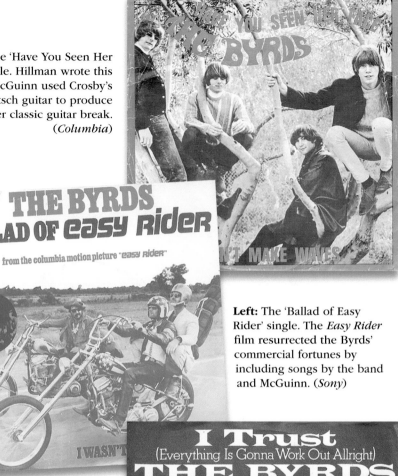

Right: The 'Have You Seen Her Face' single. Hillman wrote this and McGuinn used Crosby's Gretsch guitar to produce another classic guitar break. (*Columbia*)

Left: The 'Ballad of Easy Rider' single. The *Easy Rider* film resurrected the Byrds' commercial fortunes by including songs by the band and McGuinn. (*Sony*)

Right: The 'I Trust' single from 1971. The subtitle was McGuinn's mantra, but it proved to be ironic as they split up a year after its release. (*Columbia*)

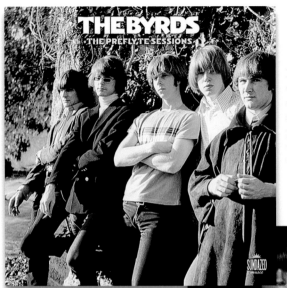

Left: *The Preflyte Sessions.*
One of a few versions
of the original *Preflyte*
album, which included
pre-Columbia demos. It was
originally released in 1969.
(*Sundazed*)

Right: *Never Before*. This 1987
compilation included unreleased
tracks from the mid-60s. Pre-
internet, it was the first time
most fans had heard these
versions. (*Murray Hill*)

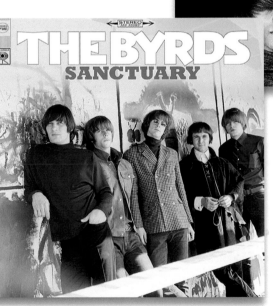

Left: *Sanctuary*. The first
volume of the career-spanning
compilations. (*Sundazed*)

This page: *Sanctuary (Vols 2, 3 and 4)*. These compilations featured previously unreleased versions and rare mixes. Gram on the front of volume 4! (*Sundazed*)

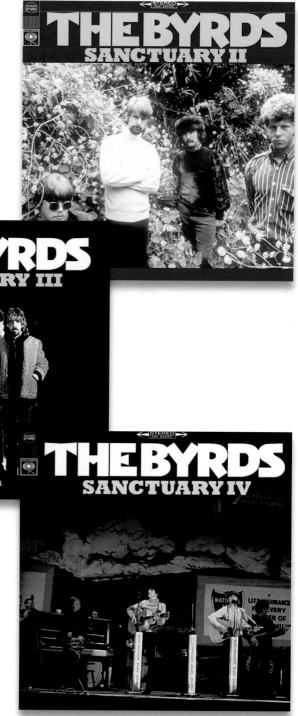

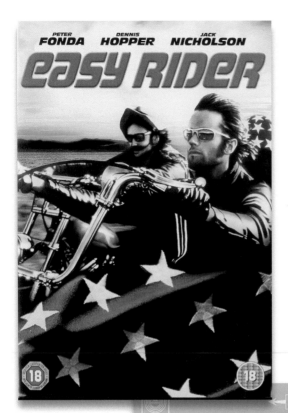

Left: *Easy Rider*. The soundrack included Byrds material, while Dennis Hopper and Peter Fonda based the main characters on Crosby & McGuinn. (*Criterion*)

Right: This poster was printed too early to include Gram Parsons. By May 1968, Byrds concerts included their new country rock repertoire. (*1960's Records*)

actually envisaged a French horn phrase in the middle part), apparently, the brass section were surprised to find no charts were provided, Crosby instead singing them the lines.

Crosby oversaw the whole recording and eventually replaced his bandmates' backing vocals with his own. The group felt it was a good song but were furious he'd gone back into the studio without telling them. Hillman reckons this is where it started to fall apart with Crosby. Up to this point, it had been fractious, but now they weren't really working together. But it doesn't change the fact that his arrangement is a triumph. With his three-part harmonies, jazzlike drumming and chorus of trumpets flying over the rapturous guitar riff, it sounds like an angelic choir on amphetamines, especially on those 'ba ba ba''s at the end of the bridge.

The single only reached 82 in *Billboard*, and didn't chart in the UK. Crosby was bitterly disappointed and later blamed Gary Usher's 'unusual' mix as a factor. Crosby also viewed it as an artistic failure. In truth, this work of great maturity is one of the band's finest moments, and is an over-looked late-1960s classic.

A warning footnote: avoid the *Never Before* version. It has re-recorded drums that were unpopular with fans. The excuse given was that they wanted to release a stereo version, but Clarke's original drumming was thought to be too weak.

In its original form, 'Lady Friend' is one of the greatest non-hit singles ever!

'Good King James' (Hemmings, Martin, McGuinn)
'Talkin' L.A.' (Hemmings, McGuinn, Hillman)
'Anathea' (Trad arr: Hemmings, McGuinn, Bond)
'War's Mystery' (Hemmings, McGuinn, Hillman)
These recordings are included because of McGuinn and Hillman's involvement with David Hemmings's 1967 MGM album *Happens:* produced by Jim Dickson. They are mild curiosity raga period pieces, but Hemming's vocals annoy after a while: particularly on 'Talkin' L.A.'. 'Anathea' is good, though, as is the version of Gene Clark's 'Back Street Mirror'.

Afterword
The album continued the band's critical reputation at a time when albums were emerging as a new art form. It predates *Sgt.Pepper's Lonely Hearts Club Band* by four months, and the band moved from being pop stars to becoming darlings of the underground. It was Crosby's favourite Byrds album, as he felt their talent was still maturing back then.

Younger Than Yesterday has good claim to be the most representative and well-loved Byrds album. It's a masterpiece (even allowing for 'Mind Gardens'). But it's not their ultimate masterpiece. That was now being worked on. As author Jon Savage told Uncut magazine in 2003: 'As always, they were going to where now is going.'

The Notorious Byrd Brothers (1968)

Personnel:
Jim McGuinn: 12-string guitar, Moog synthesiser, vocals
David Crosby: rhythm guitar, vocals
Chris Hillman: bass, mandolin, guitar, vocals
Michael Clarke: drums
Gene Clark: backing vocals
Clarence White: guitars
Red Rhodes: pedal steel
Producer: Gary Usher
Record label: Columbia, CBS (UK)
Release date: 15 January 1968
Chart position: UK: 12, US: 47
Running time: 28:28

Amid band friction, they also parted company with Dickson and Tickner, so Larry Spector started overseeing some business affairs, though the group now largely managed themselves. This increased the perception of them as a rudderless boat. The band were heading for uncertainty, or at worst, disintegration. However, in typical Byrds fashion, they looked for new creative inspiration, and started recording their absolute masterpiece. The new album could've been a disjointed mess, but instead was breathtaking!

Recording between June and December 1967, The Byrds took their pastoral psychedelic experiments even further. By mixing folk rock, country and jazz with psychedelia, and utilising Gary Usher's innovative studio techniques such as phasing, they created a chilled-out Americana psychedelia. Though the album had nostalgic themes, the overall cohesion was mainly due to Usher's production genius, where he unobtrusively faded each track into the next while retaining the songs' individual strengths. Usher was like an eager kid in the studio – full of innovative fun – and McGuinn praised his sound experiments. Usher made them feel comfortable in the studio, and was responsible for the fluidity of the record, giving the impression of a suite, by sequencing the psych, country, folk, electronic and baroque elements into one thematic statement. Unlike some other late-1960s albums, the gentle psychedelic shade keeps it from sounding dated. The album still begs to be heard uninterrupted, and while McGuinn contends that the sequencing was spontaneous, Usher was adamant that they considered the song keys in terms of how one song would segue into the next. Though the album didn't pioneer new musical directions like its follow-up or their debut, considering the fraught recording atmosphere, it has a warmth and togetherness.

During recording, McGuinn and Hillman became increasingly irritated by Crosby's egotism and King-of-the-counterculture antics – illustrated by the group's tetchy June performance at the Monterey Pop Festival, where

Crosby antagonised them further by playing with Buffalo Springfield: filling in for the missing Neil Young.

In July, the band recorded Crosby's glorious 'Lady Friend', but it ultimately suffered from poor sales. This contrasted with the success of the band's *Greatest Hits* – released on 7 August 1967 – which remains their biggest seller in their homeland. The failure of 'Lady Friend', exasperated relations further, and eventually, McGuinn and Hillman told Crosby he was impossible to work with and fired him. It wasn't done for artistic reasons, but for psychological reasons, to maintain the group: Crosby was essentially sacked due to his arrogance. He borrowed $22,500 from Monkee Peter Tork and bailed out, bought a yacht and looked for new connections to harmonise with. Terry Melcher later told a reporter that the most difficult person he ever worked with was David Crosby. When asked who the second most difficult person was, Melcher replied, 'Charles Manson!'.

Crosby considered his departure to be a shameful waste, and in terms of the songs he left behind, he had a point. The album would never have been as strong without his songs, and his vocal innovations and jazzlike inflections are missed on future Byrds recordings. They struggled to live with him and to live without him: creatively, anyway. Following Crosby's departure, Gene Clark rejoined the band, but left three weeks later. The Byrds performed 'Mr. Spaceman' on the TV show *The Smothers Brothers Comedy Hour* in October 1967, but Clark wasn't really there. Footage exists of this bored, spaced-out, zombified performance. Clark also participated in the recording sessions for some tracks, and this will be covered in the track commentaries.

Michael Clarke then quit the band over disputes about the songs they were currently recording. He left for Hawaii, happy to take a mundane hotel job. Session drummers Jim Gordon and Hal Blaine were brought in to temporarily replace Clarke in the studio, and McGuinn and Hillman were now effectively left as a duo. They triumphed in the face of adversity by producing their finest album. It should be considered that though relationships were souring in 1967, all but one of the album's nine original songs are co-writes. Ironically, the departed Crosby is still much present, with his jazz-tinged chording and flowing melodies influencing many songs.

The songs on this album and its predecessor are essential snapshots of a musical world in motion. It's a soundtrack to one of the great pop soap operas. Whatever the politics, it's a wonderful synthesis of melody and experimentation. This cowboy psych-head classic was also great for the new headphone age. Yet, for all this, it still has all the definitive Byrds sounds. And with 'Draft Morning' and their version of Goffin and King's 'Goin' Back', it has some of the band's best recordings. On 'Change Is Now' there's a moment where Byrds psychedelia merges – through an ethereal Clarence White guitar solo – with the band's coming country sound.

Though they were at a creative peak, the album suffered from having the least US sales. Though it might be recognised as a masterpiece now and regularly appears in greatest-album-ever polls (62 in *Uncut* magazine's last poll), it failed to even scrape the US top 40. But the critics were unanimous in their praise: especially the underground press. *Beat Instrumental* confirmed The Byrds as one of the two best groups in the world, while new music paper *Rolling Stone* commented that the album had a timelessness. Robert Christgau of *The Village Voice* called it their best album, and rightly felt that the occasional tracks that flawed their previous work, were now gone.

In the UK, the album achieved cult status, being their biggest album since *Mr. Tambourine Man*. *Melody Maker* prophetically asked: 'Who are they this time?'.

The front cover showed the three remaining members in a 'Wanted' pose alongside a horse: long assumed to be a slight on Crosby. But McGuinn reckons had it been a comment on Crosby; the horse would be standing the other way around! McGuinn has since conceded that Crosby should've probably been on the cover due to his contribution to the LP. Interestingly, Linda Ronstadt is photographed at the side of the same barn for the back cover of her *Hand Sown ... Home Grown* album.

Though the album was born out of chaos, McGuinn and Hillman now see it as the band's peak. It's the epitome of artistic-endeavour-conquering-adversity. Every rotation of their kaleidoscopic windows revealed a new musical idea. This last turn represented the last of the Holy Trinity of Byrds LPs. But the album was the high point in a career already with many steep peaks. As Sid Griffin told *Mojo* in 2003: 'Crosby's melodic sense, Hillman's inventive bass lines, McGuinn's lead breaks and Usher's production, were never bettered'. He's right. It's much more cohesive and simply has more great songs than their other albums. It's an astonishing feat!

'Artificial Energy' (McGuinn, Hillman, Clarke)

With its propulsive brass arrangement, this blazing anti-drug anthem was unlike anything they'd ever created. Hillman had the idea for the song (the last recorded for the album) in December 1967. (It didn't include the now departed Crosby.) The structure is unusual in that it has no chorus or bridge, and its upbeat rhythm is not really representative of the rest of the album. With its ironic lyrical nod to The Beatles' 'Ticket to Ride' its punchy soul-inflected brass and 'Taxman'-like bass patterns were influenced by The Beatles *Revolver*. The compressed horns work well, especially in contrast with the eerie piano, while Clarke's bass drum unrelentingly drives the track. He came up with the title and wrote enough of the lyric to justify a writing credit. The final line, 'I'm in jail 'cause I killed a queen' is possibly one of Clarke's lines.

The lyric concerns a drug freak who kills a homosexual in a speed-fuelled psychosis. Ironically, the song caused no stir, unlike 'Eight Miles High'. Nobody batted an eyelid, though that was possibly reflective of The Byrds no longer shifting large amounts of records or getting as much airplay.

Though it's a strong track, McGuinn felt that the gadget they used where it distorts the voices sounded too much like Donald Duck. Also, the brass is too high in the mix. And the paradoxical celebration-turned-elegy nature of the song was lost on some listeners. It's really an anti-drug song written on drugs. Speed was an interesting tool to McGuinn. He felt that if you had more energy and sustain, you could sing higher and play faster. He also felt that speed influenced the music more than weed or acid. However, there's not much evidence of this on the rest of the album.

'Goin' Back' (Goffin, King)

When Gary Usher suggested they record this Goffin/King song, the band hated the idea. Infamously, it's the song that fuelled Crosby's departure. As the band came around to the idea, Crosby still felt it was a step back musically, and lyrically trite. He called it sentimental mush. He didn't take part in the recording, as he felt his own material was being ignored. Presumably, he was in a huff since the band didn't show any interest in his new freak-out orgy tune: 'Triad'. Crosby had a point, though, as he'd reasonably suggested that they now had enough great material and needn't bother with other writers' songs. But when the band returned to the song after Crosby's departure, it was transformed into a glorious Byrds cover, in contrast to Dusty Springfield's more-wistful version.

The Byrds altered the tempo and arrangement to give the song a dreamy quality, and some of the lyric was changed. The 'No more electric trains/ No more trees to climb and toys to lend' line makes the song sound more yearning. The album's reflections on the passage from childhood to maturity were depicted musically by celestial harmonies and elegiac pedal-steel guitar. With its overly nostalgic lines, amazingly (considering the final mix includes a celeste, harp, cello, violin, piano, pedal steel and Moog), the atmosphere is rich and tender. The guitar break with simultaneous vocals is sumptuous, considering they no longer included Crosby's instinctive harmony genius. It's now thought that this is one of three tracks Gene Clark sang backing vocals on. It's also memorable for session drummer Jim Gordon's codifying drum roll near the end, before the last harmonic flourish.

This performance blends their autumnal harmonies and chiming Rickenbacker in stupendous style and is probably the closest they got to sounding like a Phil Spector production (especially on the earlier take on the CD reissue). It should've resurrected their hitmaking career, but sadly the single only peaked at 89 in *Billboard*. But it's now generally acknowledged as one of the Byrds' greatest tracks, where their baroque take on lost innocence is beautifully dyed with their sonic wisdom.

'Natural Harmony' (Hillman)

This acid-tinged harmonic gem is the album's only non-co-write. Like 'Goin' Back', it conveys longing for childhood's lost innocence and virtues. It has a trippy quality, soaked in a dreamlike atmosphere. The otherworldly jazz ambience is augmented by a Moog synthesizer underpinning the melody. It's like a microcosm of the whole album.

Hillman's bass line and McGuinn's country-influenced circular guitar patterns blend perfectly with those stony harmonies, which include musician Curt Boettcher. Even Hal Blaine's drums gently swing here, while the floating Moog contributes to a now-increasing Byrdsian blend of homely past and electronic future, providing a dripping liquid-acid lilt, thanks to Beaver & Krause (makers of the 1967 album The *Nonesuch Guide to Electronic Music*).

The Crosby-like lyric – while also being very much of its time – has a certain getting-it-together charm with lines like 'Dancing through the streets side by side/Heads thrown back, arms open wide'. It's an expression of idyllic bliss, like a psychedelic hymn of spiritual freedom. It's all very 1967 'Frisco, but The Byrds and Usher propel the song into minor-classic status with their inventiveness – never better represented than with the seamless segue into the next track. Whenever you hear the cross-fades gorgeous guitar run, it resonates in anticipation of the spine-tingling cymbal crescendo signalling the start of their next masterpiece.

'Draft Morning' (Crosby, Hillman, McGuinn)
Aaah, where do I start? This might not have the immediacy of Clark's early classics or the transformative appeal of 'Mr. Tambourine Man' or 'Eight Miles High', but when push comes to shove, this mesmerising head movie may be The Byrds' finest flight. A chapter could be written on Hillman's bass lines alone, or those dreamy vocal harmonies.

One of three Crosby songs that Hillman and McGuinn reworked, 'Draft Morning' is a magisterial career highlight. Worked on for four days in Hawaii (the album's longest unbroken stretch of recording), Hillman and McGuinn were instantly attracted to Crosby's melody, and continued writing the song. They changed some of the lyrics – as they'd forgotten them – and played their own bass and guitar parts.

A response to President Johnson sending more troops to Vietnam, the song traces the journey of a soldier, from the morning of his draft to his first combat experiences. Though Clark, Clarke and Hillman all had encounters with the draft, The Byrds generally kept quiet about their views on the war. Crosby claimed it wasn't an anti-establishment us-vs-them rant, but more a comment on a soldier dealing with the futility of people dying for a needless cause.

From the gentle cymbal intro to that melodic, undulating and gulping Hillman bass line and the eerie dreamy vocals, the song is near perfection. Firesign Theatre gunfire sound effects (combined with bugle calls) create a startling shift, working perfectly as an offbeat middle eight to evoke the eerie and deadly sound of combat, before returning to the core of those gentle, ghostly harmonies, which again includes Curt Boettcher. The bass and the understated, dulcet-toned vocals, alongside McGuinn's cyclical arpeggios and Hillman's mandolin runs, contribute to a warm groove throughout. For the best version, check out the longer CD reissue version with McGuinn's guitar picking and those gentle harmonies fully played out in a dreamy coda.

This was the first track recorded for the album after Crosby left (though album credits still refer to Croz on guitar). McGuinn and Hillman's reinterpretation is startling, with Crosby's ghostly phrasing reborn through McGuinn varying his voice. It's a tribute to Crosby's soothing, far-away vocal phrasing with its mournful message wrapped in divine beauty. I recently asked Crosby a question about this song via *Uncut* magazine – I wondered if he was still bitter about the band recording this, as he'd previously referred to it as theft and had been furious at their cavalier decision to rework the track, protesting that it was unethical to rewrite the song and take half the credit. But more than 50 years later, he felt it was water under the bridge.

With its gorgeous melody, the song is the album's centrepiece – a creative collage that probably only The Beatles or Brian Wilson could match at the time. It is a true masterpiece: a shining testament to the Byrds' glowing genius.

'Wasn't Born To Follow' (King, Goffin)
Though McGuinn was reticent to record another Goffin/King song, he knew this one had potential. Gary Usher was again a big influence here (especially with that cross-fade intro), convincing the group that it suited the album's thematic whole'.

Now divorced, Goffin and King were writing more socially-conscious material – like 'Pleasant Valley Sunday' – with a new lyric ambience, different from their Brill Building songs. In fact, this song was originally intended for The Monkees, though phased, psychedelic country was maybe a step too far from their current hit, 'Daydream Believer'. The song's non-conformist theme would eventually inform a scene in *Easy Rider*. Though the song is more about innocence and living life on your own terms, it was used to capture the spirit of freedom and rebellion, and helped the song reach a wider audience. It was also released as a single when the film was released in 1969.

Rather than replicating the slow piano-led original, they changed the melody and some lyrics, and sped the song up but kept the message and imagery of freedom intact. Producer Usher added some memorable cosmic phasing, where he used an old trick of using two tape machines at different speeds. The eastern-flavoured phased electronic break (which includes a drone effect) complements the album's ethereal feel, and runs alongside Clarence White's country picking and Rhodes' light and unobtrusive pedal steel, giving a psychedelic country-rock feel. The cosmic country vibe then explodes in the middle eight with a piercing McGuinn solo.

With the phasing and swooping as the lead guitar flies free, Simon Nicol of the UK's Fairport Convention felt this was like a Brill Building song arranged as a perfect frozen moment of free-spirited hippie ideals. He reckoned that if you wanted to know in three minutes what the 1960s were like, just listen to this track.

The song ends enigmatically with a door slamming (it wasn't even the side closer). Perhaps this was a metaphor for the counterculture's naïve flower power elements beginning to wilt, or a door being shut on the quest for materialism. Gary Usher tries to make some sense of it on the next track, which was magnificently segued into.

'Get to You' (Hillman, McGuinn)

This gorgeous fried soft rock track has an enigmatic chorus with confusing lyrics – especially 'Aaah, that's a little better'. The words have been misinterpreted – such as 'back to Roberta' – and as the lyric chronicles a trip to London, it's also ambiguous who the 'you' is. McGuinn liked it that way, as it kept things mysterious.

Gary Usher claimed the intro's enigmatic door-slamming was just a bit of fun rather than an allegorical or cryptic message. After the door slam, the 5/8 arrangement is replete with strings, and pedal steel played by Red Rhodes. It blends into a chorus with a 6/8 time signature, (allegedly, McGuinn worked with different time signatures to show Crosby how good a musician he was), and vocals through a Leslie speaker. It's a wonderfully-languid way to end side one: the best vinyl side in The Byrds' discography.

There's also confusion regarding the song's authorship. McGuinn clearly remembers writing this with Gene Clark in his house, and it was previously assumed that Hillman got the credit due to an administrative error, which was never contested. However, Hillman has claimed he partly wrote the song but doesn't remember what Gene contributed. According to John Einarson's Gene Clark biography *Mr. Tambourine Man*, it's a McGuinn/Clark co-write. Either way, it's thought Clark definitely sang backing vocals, and sideman and soon-to-be Byrds member Clarence White also appears.

Clearly, the group Big Star loved this song, as you can hear its influence on a lot of their music, especially the vocal phrasing.

'Change is Now' (Hillman, McGuinn)

Side two starts at a truly cosmic psychedelic-country juncture pointing towards their next two albums. This was the first track recorded for the album, and McGuinn's piercing psychedelic guitar break is astonishing, accentuated by Clarence White's country guitar playing. It also features wonderful David Crosby harmonies. The mystical vibe is punctuated by spiritual lyrics about living life to the full and how the whole universe is made up of music. The original title was 'Universal Mind Decoder', and it's McGuinn's revolutionary Utopian mantra about relativity and string theory!

The pumping bass with its picking motif was – surprisingly – played by Crosby, and moves through a country chorus and a mass of backwards guitar, creating a psychedelic opus. The urge to innovate was becoming contagious.

For his scorching sitar-like Fender guitar solo, McGuinn used a battery-operated record player, added an amplifier, put it in a cigar box and attached it to a walkie-talkie speaker. This created sustain that lasted for over a minute.

Clarke's driving drumming here is some of his best on record, and White's delicate Appalachian picking and understated chunky rhythm are also notable. It's a masterful fusion, mixing folk structures and acid-rock flourishes with an experimental country-rock chorus driven by pedal steel. It's another example of the group's musical continuity, as it's an older and more-advanced sibling of 'Natural Harmony', especially with the phrase 'Keep in harmony'.

The term 'Always beyond today' was often used to describe The Byrds, and was never better represented than in this song. In some ways, it's the archetypal Byrds song, as it shows folk, acid and country rock all meeting in one place. Truly cosmic country!

'Old John Robertson' (Hillman, McGuinn)
Though some Byrdmaniacs regard this as a bit of a throwaway, it was actually recorded twice. Set to a two-step country rhythm, Crosby plays bass. It's a whimsical tale of an eccentric old silent-film director from Hillman's childhood. (The earlier version was originally the B-side to 'Lady Friend'.)

The song has a certain playful, cosmic charm, and captures the mix of old and new sounds, that run throughout the record. It was originally conceived as a country song, but when a string orchestra happened to be in the studio, they were utilised for the middle section's Beatlesque baroque section. McGuinn arranged the strings, which are a contrast to the country canter of the sawing fiddle. Phasing was then added to the passage. Hillman later regretted the 'stupid' string quartet section and felt it was just posturing. I agree with Martin Orkin, who, in his book *Rivals of The Beatles,* says the unnecessary added effects were the only poor decision on the whole album. An intriguing mix featuring mandolin overdubs exists, but remains unreleased.

Compared to most of the album, this does pale slightly, but it's the sort of bass-driven bluegrass pastiche that McCartney could've written.

'Tribal Gathering' (Crosby, Hillman)
The inspiration for this harks back to Crosby's love of vocal groups like The Four Freshmen. The song examines the hippie culture Crosby had warmly embraced, and the lyric is a companion piece to 'Renaissance Fair'. Others – including McGuinn – wrongly assumed that 'Tribal Gathering' referred to Monterey, but Crosby was describing the first love-in he attended: at Elysian Park on Easter Sunday, 1967. Crosby the belligerent as a hippie, is a concept that summons a wry smile, but nonetheless, the song is pure Summer-of-Love bliss.

Drugs played a big part in The Byrds' new music, and their creative audacity in the studio was flourishing. It's impossible to avoid being hooked in straight away with the vigorous guitar groove and vocal harmonies that eventually give way to another piercing, distorted McGuinn guitar solo, and great drumming by Hal Blaine. The effervescent harmonies (including Crosby's) are absolutely stunning, giving the song a glorious jazz lilt. Though this was partly arranged by Hillman, it's essentially Crosby's song, and links back to his early relationship with unconventional chords and tunings: influenced by growing up with jazz, choral and classical music. Crosby loved jazz (his brother Ethan introduced him to it in the late-1950s), and its influence is all over this track with Crosby's 5/8 time signature and scat vocals, which sound particularly influenced by Dave Brubeck's cool jazz.

With its proto-punk riff, the incendiary heavy-rock break is like a metaphor for Hells Angels' arrival at the festival. British musician Richard Hawley was once accused of stealing the riff for his 'Down in the Woods' from The Stooges' '1969', but he took it from where that group's Ron Ashton got it from: 'Tribal Gathering'! To be fair, McGuinn probably took the riff from Bo Diddley!

The track is explorative and emblematic of The Byrds as a unit: fractious but so very creative. This finger-snapping address to the communal hippie ethos at its Utopian peak is like a frenzied jazz-rock trip with swirling sound effects. Utterly glorious.

'Dolphin's Smile' (Crosby, Hillman, McGuinn)

The last of the three songs Crosby *left* for the band anticipates the calming sea-themed songs of his various post-Byrds incarnations: like 'The Lee Shore'. It still has a period charm, with dreamy harmonies and another beautifully succinct McGuinn solo. Like the prior track, the middle section sounds like a riff The Stooges borrowed from for '1969'.

From the start, McGuinn's fingernails scratching on his Rickenbacker imitate a school of communicating dolphins, and the track effortlessly glides with his psychedelic guitar sonics and the blissful vocal harmonies (including Crosby's). Though Crosby agreed to share the publishing, he was upset that the others also got credit here, and later said the whole song was his.

These sessions – which also produced 'Tribal Gathering' and 'Triad' – were fractious, and not just between the songwriters. Michael Clarke now wanted to leave the band, as he found the new material hard to play – especially Crosby's new songs with their jazz time signatures. When recording this track, an argument ensued when Clarke couldn't get his drum part right and Crosby started taunting him. (Some of that can heard on the album's CD reissue.) Indeed, Hal Blaine eventually took over on drums, paving the way for Clarke to leave.

This daring song – which could've erred on the side of being twee – is lifted to something so serene. It's a perfect example of the creative freedom Crosby was looking for.

'Space Odyssey' (McGuinn, Hippard)

This might've sounded intriguing in 1968, but the slow tempo never really lifts it above that of a soundscape experiment with no variance from its funereal drone. With its fusion of the traditional and the future, it's a favourite of McGuinn's. There's no denying it continues the band's studio experimentation, as they were working with the new Moog synthesizer. Initially, McGuinn conceived an idea of a second disc of Moog experiments, and this was even mooted as the route the band may take next.

Inspired by Arthur C. Clarke's *The Sentinel*, 'Space Odyssey' concerns the evolution of man, with some speculation on alien involvement. McGuinn knew co-writer Bob Hippard from his folk club days.

It's an astral-folk sea shanty floating in space, and sounds otherworldly. If you listen with headphones, the left channel is mainly synth, and the right side has the modal backing. The trippy synthesizer links it to traditional British folk, and few other Byrds tracks reached so far back to the past and so far into the future.

The melodically interesting and melding fuzz guitar and twiddling Moog (only the tenth album to feature the synth) provide a spooky, unearthly atmosphere complementing the backing vocals (which possibly include Gene Clark) on the song you'd probably associate least with the original Byrd.

Unlike the previous humourous album closers, this is both ancient and novel. And though the ambitious track has dated, it defines this album's quietly pioneering frontier-crossing invention.

Connected Flights

'Old John Robertson' (Single version) (Hillman, McGuinn)

This was included as an extra to emphasise it as the better version, in terms of the LP version's effects being absent. This was actually included on the *Younger Than Yesterday* CD reissue, as it was the US B-side of 'Lady Friend', but it makes more sense placed here for comparison purposes with the album version. Less is more!

'Moog Raga' (McGuinn)

With its Eastern raga meeting electronica, this could've been the band's next sound had they not tread the country path. This crazed instrumental was going to be on the album, and was advertised as such pre-release, but was probably pulled for being too sonically similar to 'Space Odyssey'.

It's an interesting instrumental raga experiment with lots of Moog noodling, though admittedly, it would've paled against the album's other glorious tracks, and its Ravi Shankar in outer space feel is now dated. Interestingly, McGuinn bought his Moog from its inventor Robert Moog. But it came with no instructions, so McGuinn had to figure it out for himself. He also admits the melody was out of tune on this track.

'Bound to Fall' (Brewer, Mastin)

This instrumental version seemed to have been forgotten about, as it wasn't mentioned in any session notes. So it was a pleasant surprise when it was included on the *Notorious* CD reissue. Presumably, no vocal version exists, but instrumentally there's a cosmic-jig vibe going on, which – though very-much a work in progress – shows great potential. McGuinn's jazz-like guitar playing is especially fluid.

Hillman performed a version on *The Byrds American Broadcast* 2021 live CD, and he did a vocal version on the eponymous 1972 *Manassas* album. These tease the listener into wondering what the Crosby/Hillman/McGuinn-era Byrds might've done with the song, especially if they'd included the scat vocal of the Manassas arrangement. It would've been right up Crosby's street.

'Triad' (Crosby)

This is an audacious song of sexual liberation, where Crosby attempts to outline the benefits of a *ménage à trois* to a – presumably – female acquaintance. Crosby's vocals are great (something Gary Usher always liked about the track). However, it was the song that took Crosby's petulant attitude towards the band to new levels, as he saw covers of Goffin/King songs as a backwards step and more evidence of his songs being ignored, and this song failed to make it onto the album. It was the final track he cut with the group until their 1970s reunion.

McGuinn has suggested the reason the band didn't release it was because it was a bad song and not because they saw it as a tasteless hippie anthem. Hillman concurred, as he didn't think it fit into what they were doing then. Though Hillman's argument is surely a sideways reference to the lyric, since musically, The Byrds were the very broadest of churches. Crosby later admitted that *he* had spread the excuse that they thought it was tasteless, and he later recorded it live with Crosby, Stills, Nash & Young (included on *4 Way Street* in 1971) and as a demo during the *Déjà Vu* sessions. Ironically, the Byrds version is much better than any of the insipid CSNY versions. Interestingly, Jefferson Airplane adopted an ironic switch of gender context when they recorded 'Triad' for their 1968 album *Crown of Creation* (with Grace Slick on vocal).

'Flight 713' (McGuinn, Hillman)

This was first released as an extra on the *Never Before* CD compilation. The guitar pattern is lovely. It has a loose, reckless experimentation harking back to the folk-rock days, and the rhythm and lead pattern was something McGuinn took from Shel Silverstein's guitar picking.

'Flight 713' got its title from McGuinn looking at the studio clock, which said 13 minutes past seven – which is still more exciting than the track's working title, 'Song Number 2'!

'Universal Mind Decoder' (McGuinn, Hillman)

This is an early instrumental version of 'Change is Now'. Clarke liked his funky rhythm part. In fact, even Crosby liked it. He eventually played bass on 'Change is Now' itself.

The track now belongs in Byrds notoriety, as the CD reissue version has an extended take, including this instrumental workout and an argument between Crosby and Clarke. The drummer is struggling to get his drum fills right for 'Dolphin's Smile': listen for the beginning of the end of this incarnation of the group lineup!

Monterey Pop Festival Live Recordings

This was a poor Byrds set, dominated by Crosby, and it fuelled the fire that San Francisco bands were better than L.A. bands: live, anyway. Check out YouTube clips as evidence that this was a fractious and unmemorable Byrds performance. The Byrds set can be found on the *Monterey International Pop Festival* box set (except for 'I Know My Rider'): 'Renaissance Fair', 'Have You Seen her Face', 'Hey Joe', 'He Was a Friend of Mine', 'Lady Friend', 'Chimes of Freedom', 'I Know my Rider', 'So You Want to Be a Rock 'n' Roll Star'.

Afterword

Amid a general feeling of turmoil, The Byrds recorded their most expansive and greatest album – more alive with sonic adventure. Crosby's departure influenced a languid eclecticism that contributed to a more relaxed feeling of nostalgic yearning. He left behind three songs that McGuinn and Hillman arranged into three of the band's best songs, proving that the yin and yang between Crosby and the rest of the band was often invaluable. The group's lack of unity resulted in all the writers becoming prolific enough to push the band in new directions. The album represents the band at their creative zenith, and is their finest hour. Perhaps their pioneering nature prevented them from maintaining chart success, but if they'd aimed to record hits only, they'd never have been as creative. However, there's no question they lost a certain maverick spirit when Crosby left. The band's next move would have to be special.

Interlude: Callin' Me Home

Ever evolving with each successive album, McGuinn and Hillman were already looking for something new, as they didn't want to be pigeonholed. McGuinn had the idea of doing a double-album chronology of music, starting with baroque, through Appalachian country, jazz, rock 'n' roll, and ending with electronic music. But the band didn't show enough interest.

It seemed like the most natural path to follow was bluegrass, since they'd already anticipated the trend, and didn't need much convincing to investigate traditional values, as they always considered country to be part of the folk tradition. But to do this, they needed a drummer and a keyboard player. Then they met a barely-known cosmic cowboy named Gram Parsons, and together they developed the country rock genre.

Sweetheart of the Rodeo (1968)

Personnel:
Roger McGuinn: guitar, banjo, vocals
Chris Hillman: bass, mandolin, vocals
Gram Parsons: guitar, vocals
Kevin Kelley: drums
Clarence White: guitar
Lloyd Green: steel guitar
Producer: Gary Usher
Record label: Columbia, CBS (UK)
Release date: 30 August 1968
Chart position: UK: -, US: 77
Running time: 32:35

For the post-*Notorious* tour, they replaced Michael Clarke with Hillman's cousin Kevin Kelley (born California 25 March 1943), who'd played with The Rising Sons. Then Gram Parsons (born Florida 5 November 1946) was hired as keyboard player. Hillman knew him from Parsons' International Submarine Band, whose *Safe At Home* album is regarded as one of the starting points of country rock. But if Hillman and McGuinn thought they were merely hiring a piano player, they were in for a surprise. Buoyed by the band's idea to marry country and rock, Parsons began to assert his authority – his vision being to make country music hip for a younger audience and the new counterculture. He took the opportunity and was the only Byrds member to write songs for the new album.

Hillman was now playing mandolin, and McGuinn banjo. Gradually, virtuoso pedal steel and fiddle parts were added to their new repertoire of honky-tonk melancholy. The Byrds became the first *hippies* to play at the Grand Ole Opry, but were met with some heckling. Remaining stoic, they approached the new album practically, working with some of the best country musicians. The pedal steels of Lloyd Green and JayDee Maness dominate most of the songs, and also included was John Hartford, who wrote the Glen Campbell hit 'Gentle on My Mind'.

But the figure most cited as the major catalyst for the new album was Gram Parsons, the charming rich boy who is now seen as one of the major reinventors of American roots music. His increasing influence saw him briefly replace McGuinn as the band's driving force. McGuinn and Hillman gradually grew suspicious of Parsons' demands – at one point suggesting the group be billed as Gram Parsons and The Byrds. But in April 1968, McGuinn's position as head Byrd was reinforced by the new single 'You Ain't Goin' Nowhere': a Dylan song from his *The Basement Tapes* sessions.

The new album was a logical continuation of a path that already had sidetracks dating back to their 1965 cover of 'Satisfied Mind'. The Byrds weren't the only ones that came close to country either – The Monkees'

Mike Nesmith had managed to get 'Papa Gene's Blues' on the first Monkees album in late-1966, and Hillman always cites Rick Nelson as a major influence on country rock.

The Byrds appeared fearless to record a country album, as rock and country were on opposite sides of the barricade in 1968. It was unexpected, and radical at the same time. To embrace rural music was okay as a tangent, but a whole album of it was a risk for their relationship with rock fans, especially since the British Invasion had pushed traditional music into the margins. But like-minded artists were also busy *bringing it all back home*, and getting rustic was now in fashion thanks to Dylan's late-1967 LP *John Wesley Harding*, and the emergence of his old backing band The Hawks: now renamed The Band.

But just after releasing *Sweetheart*, The Byrds seemed to lose their entire audience. McGuinn felt that the band were pioneers, but with arrows in their backs. The arrows referred to both sides of the country-rock divide. The hippies thought they'd gone redneck, and the rednecks thought they were lousy hippies. The counterculture perceived the country scene's right-wing political views as the antithesis of the hippie ethos, and some fans were initially wary that they'd sold out to the enemy. The band that had produced 'Eight Miles High' two years earlier were now playing bluegrass, and had the temerity to sport short hair! Equally, the country scene was suspicious of the band's druggy image.

But in retrospect, abandoning psychedelic folk rock proved The Byrds were ahead of the game, and the album's influence slowly permeated through rock music, eventually becoming a road map for 1970s country rock. Over subsequent generations, the album became a magnet as country rock mutated into the indie-bred alternative country.

Hillman and McGuinn acknowledge it was a revolutionary record that opened the floodgates for other invading hippies seen as outrageous to the country-music establishment. Country musicians Lloyd Green and Vern Gosdin agree The Byrds were the first rock band to approach country music in such a purist way, merging country and rock to take to both audiences. McGuinn also feels the album influenced the whole Outlaw Country thing.

Parsons left the band after six months. He objected to several of his lead vocals being replaced due to 'contractual obstacles' (and the probability that Parsons was becoming too dominant), and apparently, he was incensed that the band were going to tour South Africa, as he opposed apartheid. But sources closer to the band suggest that by this stage, he was more interested in hanging out with Keith Richards in the south of France. The cosmic cowboy was gone: even before the album was released. While McGuinn appreciates that Parsons was a catalyst for their country direction, it's important to remember that Parsons was a Byrd for only a short time, and that the impression of him hijacking the group's flight is not wholly accurate. Hillman has never had enough credit for introducing country rock to the mainstream: in 1966, he was already writing songs with a country flavour.

In 1973, Parsons criticised McGuinn and Usher for making the album 'Hollywood freaky', but this is harsh. The Byrds brought their love of country music into a broader context, and in some ways, this was their most folky album up to that point.

When the album was released in August 1968 (their first mixed exclusively in stereo), the reception was inauspicious. *NME* referred to it as corny, and *Rolling Stone* called it uninvolved. However, Jon Landau later reassessed it, saying the band showed just how relevant country music really was. In *The Village Voice*, Robert Christgau acknowledged that it needed the canted approach of The Byrds, who combined respect with critical distance. The album was a slow burner with buyers, and it took a while to have an impact on the mainstream. Bear in mind that Tony Palmer's classic *All You Need Is Love* music documentary series (conceived in 1973) makes little reference to country rock: proof that the impact of *Sweetheart* took time to germinate.

But there was the ubiquitous instant reaction of fellow musicians, who saw the new rootsy sound as being visionary. Along with The Band, The Byrds' new repertoire paved the way for others who were bored with the excess of psychedelia. Crosby, Stills & Nash took a sweeter version into the mainstream, and Grateful Dead's Jerry Garcia returned to his bluegrass roots and used a pedal steel for the Dead's classic 1970 albums *Workingman's Dead* and *American Beauty* (albums that were also influenced by David Crosby's harmonies). *Sweetheart of the Rodeo* probably influenced Dylan too, as he headed to Nashville to make his *Nashville Skyline* album. Gram Parsons had a big influence on his new friend Keith Richards too, informing future Rolling Stones songs 'Wild Horses' and 'Dead Flowers'.

The album helped reintroduce a musical style that had largely been lost on the mainstream during the rock 'n' roll revolution. It's biggest influence is seen by the trail leading to The Flying Burrito Brothers and The Eagles, whose diluted iteration flew into mainstream music, their *Greatest Hits* album later becoming at one point the biggest-selling album of all time.

What hasn't matured as well is the album cover. The art dates back to a 1933 Geller and Butler advertisement that Gary Usher spotted.

Sweetheart of the Rodeo established country rock (though it doesn't have much rock). Over the next few years, The Byrds' music predicted the dusty roads their contemporaries navigated, as The Byrds' particular route mapped the lineage of many artists in the late-1960s and early-1970s.

'You Ain't Goin' Nowhere' (Dylan)

This new Dylan song was the first airing of the band's new country direction, and was proof that their great acid affair was over. Astonishingly, this glorious track was released as a single only three months after *The Notorious Byrd Brothers* came out. Now with Hillman's delicate but increasingly-distinctive tones more to the fore, it still has those classic West Coast harmonies, with some hippie swagger, but they were now augmented by Lloyd Green's joyful skipping pedal steel. Announcing a brand-new sound, it's probably the track's greatest hook: producing a real Bakersfield feel. Green was told to play 'everywhere', giving the song a floating feel. The chiming steel guitar replaces McGuinn's Rickenbacker as the lead instrument, and a subtle Gram Parsons organ track also runs through it.

There's a certain lightheartedness in McGuinn's vocal – perhaps *too* much for Bob Dylan, who noticed that McGuinn had changed the line 'Pick up your money and pack up your tent' to 'Pack up your money and pick up your tent'. No one is really sure if Dylan was miffed or just fooling around when in later performances of the song, he sang, 'Pack up your money, pick up your tent, McGuinn'!

In some ways, this track is a false representation of the album. Along with 'One Hundred Years from Now', it characterises the band's old sound more than any other track here. While it still has a rock rhythm, some of the other tracks are almost pure country. With the Dylan cover, they'd linked to their own heritage while taking it in a new direction. While 'You Ain't Goin' Nowhere' isn't the first country rock track, it's maybe the first to kick-start the movement.

'I Am a Pilgrim' (Trad: arranged by McGuinn, Hillman)
Quite possibly their most serious foray into country, this traditional bluegrass number has no rock instrumentation at all, with John Hartford's fiddle taking centre stage alongside McGuinn on banjo. Hillman remains unconvinced by his vocal, though it is respectable, as he sings with just enough conviction, compared to some McGuinn vocals that have a tongue-in-cheek tone. Hillman makes the song sound like a mountain psalm, subtly updating the old-fashioned phrasing in places, making it more listenable for a younger audience.

This is apparently one of Hillman's favourite Clarence White guitar performances, as it reminded him of the Merle Travis version he really enjoyed. Pedal-steel player JayDee Maness also liked the overall track.

Prophetically, this was the first Byrds single to miss the US chart, but albums were now viewed as artistic statements, and tracks like this were more likely to get FM airplay than AM. It was also the first Byrds' single not to have a traditional McGuinn slant in that his guitar and harmonies weren't present.

'The Christian Life' (Louvin, Louvin)
This is the album's most ironic track, though probably unintentionally. The Byrds celebrating Christianity and its virtues is a long way from the glorious Louvin Brothers' version on their 1958 *Satan Is Real* album. (Check the album cover's burning effigy of the Devil.) Parsons had always been fascinated by non-secular music, and knew many gospel songs, this being one he sourced and looked to take the lead vocal on. But McGuinn re-sung Parsons' vocal,

partly due to his former label owner Lee Hazlewood threatening legal action if they used Parson's vocal, and partly because McGuinn and Hillman were increasingly wary of Parsons' overriding influence on the album.

McGuinn took more of a method-acting approach to his vocal, which comes across as exaggerated *hick*. Though McGuinn later embraced Christianity, at this point, he had no interest in fundamentalist Hellfire lessons. Perhaps if Hillman had taken the lead, the lyric might've been minus ironic derision, and with less imitation of Parson's Southern accent.

While The Byrds' harmonic blend did justice to the Louvin's waltz, it ended up sounding like a parody instead of a faith celebration. McGuinn certainly went a little overboard with the accent, but in fairness, he was playing a part, and on the chorus, his singing is tender enough to complement the mournful, drawling harmonies. But the great vocal debate tends to undermine the magnificent pedal-steel and guitar interplay.

For the last word on the vocals, Parsons is included on the McGuinn lead-vocal mix, but is way in the background. However, the outtake with Parsons' lead vocal (many of which are on the 2003 CD Legacy reissue) is the better take and – unlike McGuinn's – has the same sincere phrasing as the Louvin Brothers' version.

'You Don't Miss Your Water' (Bell)
Soul meets country on this rework of William Bell's soul hit that's probably best known from Otis Redding's *Otis Blue* album. It's somewhat dominated by Earl Ball's edgy honky-tonk piano, and again McGuinn and Hillman replaced Parsons' lead vocal. This version is closer to William Bell's version, though Hillman says they were also influenced by the Taj Mahal version. The country ending and Earl P. Ball's roadhouse piano give a desolate barroom feel. The song is more in line with the Parsons' cosmic American music vision in that it merged country and soul, and wouldn't have sounded out of place on The Flying Burrito Brothers' magnificent 1969 album *The Gilded Palace of Sin*.

Their high harmonies are splendid – McGuinn reverting to his more-familiar vocal manner, which has more Byrds-like clarity and really floats above the song. Parsons' version (heard on the 1990 box set) is more empathetic and soulful.

'You're Still on My Mind' (McDaniel)
Parsons claimed this wasn't intended for album inclusion. But considering the 60 attempted takes (according to JayDee Maness), a lot of time and effort was invested. Written and originally performed by Luke McDaniel, Parsons was more familiar with the George Jones version, and Parsons' vocal drawl suits the sentiments, while McGuinn's harmonies are vintage Byrds. The steel guitar and honky-tonk piano perfectly suit the sad tale of a heartbroken drunk who no longer finds comfort in drinking his sorrows away. For all Parsons' protests, this is a good take: especially his vocal. More than any other song

on the album, it proves McGuinn's assertion that while he was looking for a piano player, what he got was George Jones in a sequin suit.

'Pretty Boy Floyd' (Guthrie)

Sounding like traditional Appalachian holler, this folky bluegrass take on Woody Guthrie's song works really well. McGuinn sings the folk-outlaw narrative well, foreshadowing his 1990s Folk Den website. It should be no surprise that he was comfortable singing this, as he sings with great ebullience, fully engaged in his role as folk storyteller. Like in some of the band's early Dylan and Goffin/King covers, they changed or removed some lines, such as not referring to paying off mortgages.

The old-time backing is driven by sawing fiddle, banjo, mandolin and double bass, with John Hartford's understated fiddle particularly demonstrating the traditional roots. Apparently, McGuinn originally attempted the banjo part here but wasn't satisfied, so Hartford took over; his influence converting it into a 2/4 bluegrass hoedown. Although Hartford is all over this track, hats off to Hillman for his mandolin work at the end – he's very much in his bluegrass comfort zone.

Being another track on the compilation *The Original Singles: 1967-1969*, it took about six months to convince my teenage brain that this was definitely the same group who recorded 'My Back Pages' and 'Renaissance Fair' on side one of that same 1982 compilation!

'Hickory Wind' (Parsons, Buchanan)

This is the album centrepiece, and arguably the greatest song Parsons ever wrote. It's certainly his signature song. Its roots may go back to his older song 'Brass Buttons', which he wrote about his mother in 1965 when his songs took a more-personal country approach. He listened to Buck Owens, Merle Haggard, George Jones and The Louvin Brothers, and especially empathised with their homesick, melancholy songs.

Even if they've never been there, the yearning nostalgia makes the listener feel homesick for the Carolina pines. Parsons wrote the first verse and chorus on a train from Florida back to L.A., and his friend Bob Buchanan helped with verses two and three. The nostalgia for lost innocence probably comes from Parsons being a lonely kid (Hillman and Parsons lost their fathers to suicide when they were 16 and 12, respectively), and the yearning lyric is sung with a moving sadness evoking a powerful image.

Parsons is lead vocalist here, as McGuinn couldn't sing it tenderly enough. But his sumptuous overdubbed falsetto harmonies *were* used, though they sound more like a female. Also, if you listen closely, someone has a coughing fit just as Parsons starts singing.

With Lloyd Green's underpinning, whispering pedal steel (which evokes sadness more appropriately here than on any other track) and Hartford on fiddle, the waltz also includes a moaning dobro and Parsons on (slightly sloppy) piano. While the piano climbs, the sighing violins add a melancholy weariness, and there's a lovely, soothing slide break from Green. McGuinn's guitar adds maximum emotional effect; the heartbreaking music conveying how the simple city life is no longer attainable, and yearning for the simple rural life is all that remains.

In 2002, blind folk singer Sylvia Sammons alleged authorship of the song, claiming she'd played it at coffee houses in 1963. But it later emerged that she was 12 at the time. Bob Buchanan and Chris Hillman had always refuted her claims anyway.

'Hickory Wind' should've been a single. Why the record company thought 'I Am a Pilgrim' made a better single, is curious. Did they fear Lee Hazlewood might cause trouble if they'd had a hit with Parsons singing it? Or did they want a single sung by an original Byrd? Also, the band probably didn't want to give Parsons more exposure due to his ego. Emmylou Harris reckons that Parsons' ballad proved he was a country boy, and that the longing was a deep part of what he was trying to convey.

'One Hundred Years From Now' (Parsons)

'Hickory Wind' might be Parsons' best song, but this reflection on attitudes 100 years hence comes close to it. The mood is country, but there's a pounding rock rhythm, and those harmonies really fly. Clarence White plays electric guitar, with Lloyd Green again in great steel-guitar form – boy, does he know how to kick off an intro! Green later said that working on *Sweetheart* was one of the best experiences of his life: high praise from a veteran of over 10,000 sessions.

Though Gram envisaged something a bit more soulful, this track is, for some the closest to his vision of cosmic American music. You can certainly hear alternative country's DNA right here – by uniting musics that had no previous affinity with each other, it was a model for other bands. It recalls The Byrds' earlier vocal harmonies, and is emblematic of this album being a nod to the past in the country-folk idiom, yet it simultaneously looks forward. Being more percussive, it's closer to country rock than the rest of the album.

McGuinn's vocal and the group's backing harmonies replaced Parsons' lead vocal. Both the Parsons and McGuinn renditions are great, but McGuinn's vocal is underrated, especially in its melancholy. Parsons' more-soulful version can be found in the 1990 box set and the CD reissue, but it has no background harmonies, which I miss.

I prefer the Byrds songs that have a country-rock veneer to their pure country songs, and this is exuberant old-Byrds-meets-new-Byrds, and a song that set the scene for 'Sin City' on The Burrito's *Gilded Palace of Sin* album.

'Blue Canadian Rockies' (Walker)

A song that goes back to pre-rock-'n'-roll days, this has a Hillman vocal and McGuinn backing vocals. Written by Cindy Walker, songs of longing like this still chimed with country fans in the 1960s. Hillman knew the song from Gene Autrey's hit version which was in the western movie *Blue Canadian Rockies* starring Autry and Champion the Wonder Horse! The arrangement is decent, and Hillman's understated vocal never becomes cloaked in melodrama. However, he doesn't sound quite comfortable singing the song. His delivery doesn't entrance the listener like that of Parsons' 'Hickory Wind'. The harmonies are slightly subdued, but this is possibly because Autry's version had a histrionic choir, and The Byrds wanted their interpretation to be different.

'Life in Prison' (Haggard, Sanders)

Previously a warm-up song, Parsons was disappointed that the group didn't record a better version. The style doesn't work – it's far too jaunty, sounding almost merry, especially compared to Haggard's tormented rendition.

Parsons sings lead, and he wouldn't have included this on the album if it hadn't been written by Haggard, who he greatly admired. Maybe he wanted the song to sound a little tougher, as it has no warm Byrds harmonies. However, the echoey sound of the steel guitar, when it comes in just after the intro, is great.

Hillman has been critical of the subject matter (alcohol, murder, musings on death) in relation to Parsons, claiming it was a silly song to sing for a 22-year-old kid with a trust fund. Country singer Dwight Yoakam later echoed Hillman's sentiment regarding the folly of singing lines like 'I'll do life in prison for the wrongs I've done'. However, the idea that a singer has to have lived any song they sing is absurd – and these attitudes ignore Parsons' family history of alcoholism, insanity and suicide anyway. Maybe all that's missing from Parsons' take is the vocal dignity that only age or experience could bring.

In terms of Parson's annoyance with this version, Gary Usher said the track list was the best tracks from the material on offer: a rare time where I'd disagree with Usher. The track seems at odds with later-released *Sweetheart* outtakes. If the band were unhappy with takes like this, they could've used a track like 'Pretty Polly'.

'Nothing Was Delivered' (Dylan)

This is where country shuffle meets weird Americana. Hillman received Dylan's *Basement Tapes* version in the post. They wanted to include a couple of Dylan songs to give the album an element of the contemporary. Thinking the song had something, Hillman approached McGuinn.

The song has been interpreted as a prophetic comment on the shallow counterculture, though Hillman and McGuinn chose this and 'You Ain't Goin' Nowhere' as the most appropriate Dylan songs to represent the album. The group used the rejected second take as their template rather than the acetate version.

The track has a great McGuinn vocal, making sure he falls short of parody. His phrasing has more empathy than Dylan's, but retains the menacing tone. Kelley plays this as country rock, especially when everything merges on the throbbing chorus. As usual, Green's glorious steel guitar playing is a highlight, and Parsons is on piano and organ. But for all the clever rhythmic changes, the damning hippie-dream subject matter doesn't particularly fit the album. Also, it's one of their more-uninteresting Dylan covers, and ends the album in a rather flat fashion.

Connected Flights
'Reputation' (Hardin)
This is a lame attempt at a not-particularly-exciting song. Tim Hardin had a great songbook, but this isn't as good as some of his other songs, such as 'Black Sheep Boy' or 'Reason To Believe'. Besides the instrumental break, there's not much of a country feel, and it probably would've felt out of place on the album anyway. Parsons' vocal suggests he didn't have much conviction for the song either. A bit tongue in cheek, maybe, but if they were going to cover a Hardin song on a country-rock LP, why not try a country or bluegrass cover of 'Tribute To Hank Williams'?

'Lazy Days' (Parsons)
Parsons had recorded this with The International Submarine Band the previous year, and later cut it for *Burrito Deluxe* with The Flying Burrito Brothers. Never really considered a contender for *Sweetheart of the Rodeo* (it's too similar (and inferior) to 'Six Days on the Road'), this Chuck Berry-influenced track only appeared on *Sweetheart* CD reissues.

Essential for completists, the CD reissue has an alternate take with a nice guitar run throughout, but it's still all a bit unremarkable.

'Pretty Polly' (Arr. by McGuinn, Hillman)
This Appalachian standard should've been on the album, though it's quite folky and McGuinn plays his Rickenbacker, so perhaps they felt it wasn't the right vibe. However, the subject matter of murder is certainly a shoo-in for the album's macabre themes.

McGuinn's vocal is double-tracked, and the CD reissue has an interesting alternate take with the banjo high in the mix, and less Rickenbacker. Country artists like The Dillards have recorded the song, as did McGuinn later on *Cardiff Rose*.

'All I Have Are Memories' (Hewitt, Ledford)
Clarence White lends some brilliant fingerpicking clout, but new drummer Kelley delivers a weak lead vocal, so they could've used an instrumental mix instead. Or maybe they could've made it decent by having Parsons or McGuinn sing it.

Afterword

Chris Hillman said it best: 'The Byrds invented country rock, The Flying Burrito Brothers perfected it, and The Eagles took it to the bank'. The Byrds were the first mainstream rock act to embrace country music across a whole album, and over 55 years, *Sweetheart of the Rodeo* has certainly done more to shape country rock than most records like it.

With the band being the first folk and acid rockers, it's natural that by the time everyone caught up, the band returned to their country sound. The album was a catalyst for the country/rock/folk cross-pollination that reverberated through the 1970s singer-songwriter movement, the 1990s roots-influenced alt-country movement and beyond. The album is also the last pioneering one by one of America's greatest bands. If they'd split after its release, their album legacy would've been at least 50% revolutionary music.

But now they were at a crossroads, and had new recruitments and musical directions to consider.

Dr. Byrds & Mr Hyde (1969)

Personnel:
Roger McGuinn: 12-string guitar, vocals
John York: bass, backing vocals
Clarence White: guitars, backing vocals
Gene Parsons: drums, backing vocals
Lloyd Green: pedal steel
Producer: Bob Johnston
Record label: Columbia, CBS (UK)
Release date: 5 March 1969
Chart position: UK: 15, US: 153
Running time: 34:25

Gram Parsons only lasted six months in the band, but his influence was enormous. He seemed to gain the most from the brief union, forming The Flying Burrito Brothers and joining The Rolling Stones' world of debauchery. In contrast, The Byrds were in turmoil. With their tour of South Africa imminent, they were forced to take on roadie Carlos Bernal as substitute rhythm guitar player. Yes, the roadie! Unsurprisingly, the tour was a disaster – the band made anti-apartheid comments from the stage, which went down badly.

After the tour – in July 1968 – McGuinn and Hillman recruited session guitarist and former Kentucky Colonel Clarence White (born Clarence Joseph LeBlanc, in Maine, 7 June 1944) as a permanent member. Though tragically, he was killed by a drunk driver in 1973, White's influence on the band was profound. He never showboated, and was a born sideman, bringing sizzling guitar skills and a deep understanding of country and bluegrass, developing a playing style that others followed. He was Americana's Jimi Hendrix – effectively changing bluegrass by bringing rock-'n'-roll energy to a traditional form.

White became the longest-serving Byrd after McGuinn, and was a crucial factor in the band's early-1970s commercial renaissance. McGuinn said White had his own style that was a synthesis of all the things he'd heard. He never played anything vaguely weak, and was always driving into the music, which pulled the band up.

Shortly after joining the band, White persuaded the pair to bring in former Nashville West colleague Gene Parsons (born California 4 September 1944) on drums. White and Parsons then developed the B-Bender: a shoulder strap with a rod at the back of the guitar, allowing the ability to bend the notes on the B string.

Sadly, the new lineup lasted less than a month. Hillman had become frustrated with Larry Spector's mishandling of group finances and quit to join Gram Parsons in forming The Flying Burrito Brothers.

But only two weeks later, work began on a new Byrds album: *Dr. Byrds & Mr. Hyde* with producer Bob Johnston. After hiring young bassist John York (born

John York Foley, 3 August 1946 in New York) from The Gene Clark Group, the sessions saw McGuinn attempt to merge previous harder-edged psych rock with their new country-rock direction, giving the album a schizophrenic feel: hence its title. In some ways, this echoed not only the band's schizophrenic career, but the late 1960s itself – when peace-and-love vibes were giving way to demonstrations against war and corrupt political regimes.

Despite eroding record sales, they were booked solid. They were a top attraction, particularly in San Francisco's psychedelic ballrooms. At this point, they also began picking up good concert reviews.

But the group were disappointed with the finished album, and distanced themselves from it, blaming Johnston's production. While this might have some credence, it's also a bit disingenuous, as the material wasn't that strong, to begin with: certainly compared to previous albums. Interestingly, *Preflyte* was issued at this time, and though it was recorded in 1964, it outsold *Dr. Byrds* in the US, peaking at 84.

Dr. Byrds & Mr. Hyde is the only Byrds album where McGuinn sings lead on every track. But reviews were mixed, and it became their lowest-charting US album, though it fared much better in the UK, where it attracted mostly good reviews. John Peel also promoted it there on his influential BBC radio show *Top Gear.*

According to *NME*, this was The Byrds pushing further into country music with a Band-like feel, and *Melody Maker* praised their contrasting countrified sounds. But over the years, the album's reputation has waned, save for White's great guitar work.

The album cover typography had *Dr. Byrds* in a computerised font, and *Mr. Hyde* in an old Wild-West style. It was the perfect visual illustration of the album's schizophrenic nature. The cover was also a nod to the *Younger Than Yesterday* images of old and new Byrds worlds merging.

While the new band seemed to work as a live unit, it gained little momentum in the studio, though it is a decent album. But had Gary Usher been available, he could've added some graceful segues to smooth out Johnston's clumpy transitions from rock to country, and Usher certainly would've had McGuinn's guitar higher in the mix.

The public first heard the new material with the 'Bad Night at the Whiskey' single, which teased audiences with a new blues-rock sound.

'This Wheel's on Fire' (Dylan, Danko)
The album opens with Clarence White's ferocious psychedelic fuzz guitar, and though he complained he was never comfortable with bluesy tracks, his reverberated blues guitar really rocks here. The song has a menacing, apocalyptic feel, especially on White's burning solo and the incendiary synthesizer blast near the end. McGuinn's vocal is more bitter than those by Dylan or The Band's Rick Danko, as if McGuinn knows the end of the world is nigh.

Gene Parsons said his snare skin was so loose on this, it was like hitting a paper towel. Producer Johnston had tuned it so the snare head hung over the drum, and the resulting heavy-rock sound was like nothing heard on a Byrds track before.

This was the third Dylan song The Byrds covered from what would later become *The Basement Tapes*, and had played it live as far back as May 1968 in Rome. As enjoyable as this version is, the band's Dylan covers used to be trendsetting but now followed the pack, certainly in comparison to The Band's glorious version.

'Version one' – which appears on the CD reissue – is Clarence White's preferred take, as he was never comfortable with his paying on the released version. He's right – 'Version One' is looser, while the album version tries too hard to sound nasty like the single 'Bad Night at the Whiskey'. Also, the 'Version One' chorus harmonies are much less ominous and echoey than those on the album version.

Byrdtrivia – check out YouTube footage of them playing this on *Playboy After Dark*. McGuinn is clearly stoned during the interview with Hugh Hefner.

'Old Blue' (Arranged and adapted by McGuinn)

The album's schizophrenic feel is first felt with this upbeat take on the country and western traditional about a much-missed dog: originally titled 'Old Dog Blue'. It's arranged similarly to Bob Gibson's 1961 version, as McGuinn saw him playing the song in the Chicago folk clubs. Prior to the Byrds' version, former manager Jim Dickson produced a version by The Dillards.

The Byrds' version has great vocal harmonies, and it's the first track to feature the sound of Parsons' and White's string bender. Emblematic of the band's new direction, the take is much more country than the mournful folky versions by Joan Baez and Pete Seeger, which are laments compared to this more-celebratory take. It's only really let down by those hokey handclaps that dominate too many verses and instrumental passages.

The Byrds played this live into the next decade, and there's YouTube footage of this from their 1970 Dutch Woodstock performance.

'Your Gentle Way of Loving Me' (Paxton, Guilbeau)

This was written by two former colleagues of Gene Parsons, and Parsons and Gib Guilbeau had released the song as a single in 1967. But McGuinn still took the lead vocal, as he felt the public might be confused if new members took lead vocals so soon. He sang it well, with a gentle folk-rock feel, cosy harmonica, and outstanding guitar work from White. Another schizophrenic edge is added to the album with the reverberated ending – probably the track's most interesting part, being preceded by a pastoral passage.

But this represents the start of The Byrds needing more control of the songs they were recording, or the reduced time they spent on arranging them. Prior to this, a lot of their less-appealing tracks could be forgiven for being failed –

if admirable – experiments. But by 1969 – with fewer quality tracks – lethargy was showing.

'Child of the Universe' (Grusin, McGuinn)

Written with pianist Dave Grusin, this was included in the counterculture film *Candy*. Though McGuinn pragmatically says the song was appropriate for the film, it's curious he's never played it live, as it features his typical themes of the cosmos and the universe. It's not a favourite of many Byrds fans, and admittedly it suffers from clumpy drums and too much reverb. But it's decent enough in places – mainly the bridges as opposed to the verses.

While McGuinn sings with conviction, there's a missed opportunity when the instrumental break peters out after about five seconds, which is a shame, as those five seconds are great, with a different guitar sound. At the very least, space should've been found for a great piercing McGuinn or White guitar break. The end call-and-response vocals work well too, but again leave us too soon. Oh, for a Gary Usher to sort these things out.

The film version added orchestration which didn't really work, as it submerged some of the vocal.

'Nashville West' (Parsons, White)

This instrumental stage favourite features the string bender, and was named after a White and Parsons band from their pre-Byrds days. It also refers to a California club where Nashville West had a residency.

This version is raucous – especially the square-dance fracas towards the end – and was based on 'Hong Kong Hillbilly', which White also performed in the mid-1960s. It mixes a Bakersfield sound with bluegrass, and is often seen as White's instrumental showcase with its five-finger picking, which regularly left audiences astonished. The song worked best live, as the studio version sounds a bit rushed.

The CD reissue has an alternate, less raucous and better take, but White and Parsons preferred their theme tune as performed by the band it was named after.

'Drug Store Truck Drivin' Man' (McGuinn, Parsons)

This was written back in May 1968, and recorded in October that year. It was too late for inclusion on *Sweetheart* though – a shame, as it outshines some of that album. It first appeared as the B-side to 'Bad Night at the Whiskey'.

It's a classic, bitter country waltz, ridiculing combative country music DJ Ralph Emery, who the band had incurred the wrath of when they appeared on his Nashville radio show. He ridiculed them throughout the interview and proclaimed his dislike for 'You Ain't Goin' Nowhere'. The incident duly inspired Gram Parsons and McGuinn to write a sarcastic and condescending response to this experience. The song's truck-driving references relate to truck-driver-product adverts Emery used to play. Sadly, the confrontational lyric probably didn't irk any country-music rednecks too much, given this was the same year Merle Haggard's hippie-baiting 'Okie From Muskogee' was hugely popular in the States.

Though the song sounds like a vicious parody – and Ralph Emery was an outrageously confrontational redneck (hence the Ku Klux Klan jibe) – there's a real country authenticity with a catchy Nashville groove, and Lloyd Green on pedal steel.

As the only song Parsons and McGuinn wrote together – and with probably the wittiest of all Byrds lyrics – it's a grand ole feat! Emery never forgave them, as he mentioned it to Hillman whenever they met, even though Hillman had nothing to do with writing the song.

'King Apathy 111' (McGuinn)

McGuinn had become wary of the band being purely a country rock act, as that diminished his influence, and in some ways, this song was a microcosm of the album. It's about moving from an urban to a rural lifestyle, combining hard-edged blues (with light distortion) and country elements. It's also a comment against the world's late-1960s apathy (a strange concept 55 years later, considering this was recorded during various protest movements and political unrest), where McGuinn sings about moving to the country in fear of his life.

There's some superb, hefty McGuinn and White guitar interplay before the chorus flies into a country domain. In fact, this could've been a better single choice than the chorus-free 'Bad Night at The Whiskey'.

An album highlight, it was one of the first tracks recorded for the album, and now sounds Tom Petty-esque.

'Candy' (McGuinn, York)

This was written for the *Candy* soundtrack but apparently turned down because John York was an unknown writer (strange given that co-writer McGuinn was well known), so 'Child of the Universe' was chosen instead. This is one of the album's stronger tracks, and utilises more of the acid-country guitar sound. In retrospect, 'Candy' would've been better for the soundtrack.

Some critics refer to it very negatively, but I think they're being harsh. Granted, it's not vintage Byrds, but the guitars and vocals are more than decent enough to lift it from mediocrity, and the guitar solo works much better than the underdeveloped middle section of 'Child of the Universe'. The return of the haunting acid guitar at the end codifies the track's instrumental intent.

'Bad Night at the Whiskey' (McGuinn, Richards)

Released in January 1969, this was the album's first single. Remember, *Sweetheart* was released only the previous August. Already they were heading for another new sound, and if this was a taster of a tougher rhythm and heavier rock sound, it was really promising. It's included on *The Original*

Singles: 1967–1969, Volume 2. It's amazing to think that all the folk rock, psychedelia, bluegrass, blues rock and even gospel on that compilation was recorded in less than two years. The single mix is actually better, as the guitar solo is higher in the mix.

McGuinn's Subud friend Joey Richards wrote the lyric, which was given sinister-sounding harmonies and a great, ghostly guitar groove from White that drives the track in a slow-motion 'Purple Haze' fashion. This mordant track is also interesting in that it has no chorus and because they don't sing the title anywhere. Though the song reflects on a bad show at the Whisky A Go Go club, the lyric doesn't give any specific examples of a bad *Byrds* night: rather, it's an anonymous band (hence the misspelling of 'Whiskey').

Sadly, they never pursued this type of rock groove further, though those driving Gene Parsons drum fills became a feature of future Byrds recordings.

'Medley: My Back Pages/B. J. Blues/Baby What You Want Me to Do' (Dylan, McGuinn, Parsons, White, York, Reed)

The tradition of bizarre closing tracks is revisited here, but this is an uninspired attempt to showcase the band's new sound. They played this medley well in concert, where it was sometimes part of a longer jam, including Miles Davis' 'Milestones'. However, 'My Back Pages' minus the magisterial jangle of their mercurial studio cut, doesn't work, and it sits alongside a perfunctory run-through of Jimmy Reed's blues classic 'Baby What You Want Me to Do' and an uncredited update of 'Hold It', which they used to play before a break between sets.

Chosen to highlight the new-look Byrds' more dynamic live sound, in retrospect, the track seems like a lazy way to end the album, and suggests a lack of material. The bonus-track version on the CD reissue is a lot looser, so check that out instead.

Connected Flights
'Stanley's Song' (McGuinn, Hippard)

There's nothing to see here, really, and this was understandably an unused track. Considering it's The Byrds, the guitar solo is barely worth listening to. At best, this folky homage to Stanley Kubrick is a demo that needs a lot of work.

Previous Byrds outtakes suggest that plenty of good stuff had been left off albums. But recording two albums a year (in 1968 and 1969 anyway) was taking its toll, based on some included tracks and the poorer ones justifiably omitted.

'Lay Lady Lay' (Dylan)

In May 1969, the band released a version of this Dylan song as a single, which reached 132 in the USA but didn't chart in the UK. It's a tale of producer Bob Johnston's bad decision-making. The first 10 seconds of the single tell you all you need to know. Without the band's knowledge, Johnston overdubbed the female choir, and the band were so incensed by the gauche and unnecessary addition, that they rehired Terry Melcher as their producer. It's a mystery why they continued working with producer Johnston in the first place, as they were dissatisfied with his work on the *Dr. Byrds* album, and it's no surprise the single received lukewarm reviews.

McGuinn played an advance copy for Dylan. But even without the choir, it was a trudge compared to Dylan's soon-to-be-definitive version, which would appear on his *Nashville Skyline* album. Minus the overbearing strings, this version is better than the one with the choir. The acoustic guitars are much louder and work better. (You can find this on the 1990 box set and the CD reissue.)

'Medley (Turn! Turn! Turn!/Mr. Tambourine Man/Eight Miles High)'(Adapted, music by Seeger/Dylan/McGuinn, Crosby, Clark)
'Close Up the Honky Tonks' (Simpson)
'Buckaroo' (Morris)
'Sing Me Back Home' (Haggard)
These were all on *Live at the Fillmore – February 1969*, released in 2000. Apart from an animated 'Buckaroo', these are all fairly standard versions, and the Burritos version of 'Close Up the Honky Tonks' is better.

'Blue Suede Shoes' (Live) (Perkins)
Played live from late-1968, this is another unremarkable version of a rock-'n'-roll standard. McGuinn's grating vocals don't work, and even White's guitar seems to strangle Perkin's classic. It's included on releases like *Byrds On A Wing*, which should be avoided as they're multi-CD packages with much post and non-Byrds material.

Afterword
While it's still an interesting listen, there's a lot of filler on this album – something that became common on future Byrds albums. It continues their country-rock experiments, and there's a harder-edged nod to their acid haze. But while some of the new blues rock suggests a band with renewed energy, there's no doubt that some of the songs are tired and quickly recorded.

Meanwhile, a new low-budget movie called *Easy Rider* featured The Byrds on its soundtrack, and the film informed the title track of their next album.

Ballad of Easy Rider (1969)

Personnel:
Roger McGuinn: 12-string guitar, synthesizer, vocals
John York: bass, vocals
Clarence White: lead guitar, vocals
Gene Parsons: drums, guitar, banjo, vocals
Producer: Terry Melcher
Record label: Columbia, CBS (UK)
Release date: 10 November 1969
Chart position: UK: 41, US: 36
Running time: 33:55

The band replaced producer Bob Johnston with Terry Melcher for the new album. It had a softer edge and a warmer pastoral country-rock sound. It consisted mainly of covers and traditional songs, and all band members got at least a lead vocal. Part of the reason for this was that McGuinn had started writing (and saving) songs with his friend Jacques Levy for a stage musical idea based on the Ibsen play *Peer Gynt*. (More about this in the next chapter.)

The varied material suggests a sprawling selection, but it was a more-cohesive album than *Dr Byrds*. The band sounded tighter, and Clarence White's guitar work was fast becoming a new Byrds trademark and a huge influence on their growing reputation as a live act. This album was more laid-back and wistful. Radio ads for the album referred to it as a message for loneliness and a counterpoint to the I'm-hipper-than-you narrative of recent times.

The music may not be particularly affecting, but it's sincere enough: certainly more than the last album. In retrospect, there's something of a comforting post-Woodstock feel (though The Byrds didn't appear). The festival's euphoric vibes were still being felt by the industry and younger music fans, and with Altamont ending the decade on a bummer, maybe the appeal was one of escape.

At this stage of their career, comparisons with past glories were being made. But it's clear this version of the band was less interested in creating classic albums, and more geared towards using albums to sell concert tours and increase their live reputation, or even – in McGuinn's case – their side-project work.

Prior to the album's release, John York was asked to leave the band. He'd become disillusioned with his role, as he wasn't keen on playing old songs from before he joined. Though they were becoming a successful live act, they were now looking for their third bass player in just over a year, and York was eventually replaced by previous Skip & Flip duo member Skip Battin (Born Ohio, 18 February 1934). His appointment marked the group's last personnel change until after their *final* album in 1972. In retrospect, it's a shame York didn't hang around, as the band would've avoided recording some of Battin's below-average songs.

The Byrds' association with the *Easy Rider* film (which featured 'Wasn't Born to Follow' and solo Roger McGuinn takes of 'It's Alright Ma', I'm Only Bleeding' and 'Ballad of Easy Rider') helped the album's success. But critical reception was lukewarm, with *Jazz & Pop* magazine claiming the album was pleasant but not moving. They also harshly added that the Byrds of *Fifth Dimension, Younger Than Yesterday* and *The Notorious Byrd Brothers* had flown: a rather obvious but unfair comparison. *Rolling Stone* suggested that while the new album was like a visit with old friends, it exhibited some new sounds that only intermittently worked.

The awful cover has an out-of-focus shot of Gene Parsons' father, though the art department argued it represented this generation's search for freedom. At least the back cover was more interesting, as the sleeve notes were written by long-term friend, actor Peter Fonda.

Though the title track and 'Gunga Din' are the only genuine Byrds classics here, their popularity was increased thanks to the *Easy Rider* soundtrack, which had little to do with the album besides the title track. There was also the possibility that fans who never accepted the band's dalliance with country rock, had returned, since the album relied less on it. It's a pity McGuinn didn't foresee the return to commercial success, as he might've written more songs for the album.

'Ballad of Easy Rider' (McGuinn)

Easy Rider producer Peter Fonda put his old friends back on the map by including a version of this on the soundtrack – unsurprising, as it's assumed Fonda's character was based on McGuinn, and Dennis Hopper's based on Crosby.

Bob Dylan wrote some words on a napkin, and told Fonda to give it to McGuinn, as he'd 'know what to do with it'. McGuinn turned the introductory lines into a tasteful folk lament. Written primarily by McGuinn, Dylan apparently didn't want credit as he didn't like the end of the film, and it's not the group's recording used in the film, but McGuinn's acoustic version. But the band version was the album's first single – released in October 1969, reaching 65 in the US.

The album version has spare fingerpicked guitars and tasteful strings, sounding similar to Harry Nilsson's version of 'Everybody's Talkin'', where the gentle, meandering guitar is offset by beautiful orchestration.

However, the alternate CD reissue version with less-prominent orchestration is the best, and has some fine Clarence White picking in the break. It's a song for a hippie sundown; a happy medium between the Byrds and McGuinn versions. It encapsulates the hippie-idyll ethos for a return to simpler things.

Byrdfact: The film scene where Phil Spector carries out a drug deal was shot at the same location near LAX where Crosby and McGuinn used to hang out in their pre-fame days.

'Fido' (York)

This is the only Byrds' song credited solely to John York, and features his only lead vocal on the album. The lyric likens the writer's lonely life away from home to that of a stray dog.

Including a brief drum solo, it's one of the album's low points. York's voice grates a bit, and though musically it's a quirky stab at R&B, it's an admirable failure. Without McGuinn much in evidence, it doesn't really sound like The Byrds, but a tired band running out of ideas. McGuinn didn't like it much, and York disliked the vocal effect Melcher put on.

York left the band soon after, McGuinn suggesting that York's wife didn't like him being on tour so much. But the official reason York gave was that he didn't like playing the older material, so this song's inclusion was maybe an early compromise for him.

'Oil in My Lamp' (Trad: arranged by Parsons, White)

Gene Parsons was particularly influential in this Baptist children's hymn being recorded. He and White had sung it on the school bus. It was White's first lead vocal since his Kentucky Colonel days, and his nasal vocal is surrounded by earnest group harmonies. It's taken in a slower tempo than they used to sing it but with a rock feel. Thankfully the track never crosses the line into Christian rock. The shorter, more-upbeat outtake that appeared on the CD reissue and 1990 box set is better, as it has a more-country vocal and folky guitar backing.

This is a decent version, but again represents the beginning of the band (especially McGuinn) running out of song ideas.

'Tulsa County Blue' (Polland)

This song, written by Pamela Polland of the soft folk-psych band Gentle Soul, was originally a hit for June Carter (under the title 'Tulsa County'). John York suggested the band do it, despite Melcher owning the sheet-music copyright. Though York sang it in concert, McGuinn sung on this recording. Interestingly, York turned down Melcher's offer to acquire the publishing for 'Fido', and this might've influenced Melcher's decision to get McGuinn to sing here: such were band politics at the time.

The track highlights Clarence White's string bender, and includes fiddle player Byron Berline, who White introduced to the band as the 'world champion fiddle player'. The pair trade licks very successfully here.

The John York vocal version is on the CD reissue, but adds nothing new. In any case, with too many non-McGuinn lead vocals, the album would've struggled to sound like The Byrds at all.

'Jack Tarr the Sailor' (Trad: arranged by McGuinn)

Unlike the space-age sea shanty 'Space Odyssey' on *Notorious*, this shanty was sung in an Irish accent. It shouldn't really work, but this shimmering cover is an album highlight. It goes back to McGuinn's Gate of Horn concert days, where he learned many British folk songs.

This arrangement sounds like the band emulating the traditional, merged with the new folk rock of Fairport Convention's *Liege and Lief* album that year. The arrangement is not unlike 'I Come and Stand at Every Door' on *Fifth Dimension,* but it works better. This mournful take is better suited to McGuinn's almost risible accent (allegedly recorded drunk one night). It also has a nice gumbo of banjo, Moog synth and loping guitar lines.

Of course, it now makes even more sense in the context of McGuinn's Folk Den project.

'Jesus is Just Alright' (Reynolds)

This is the band's first and best attempt at gospel (or near gospel). Parsons knew this song from the Art Reynolds Singers, and in December 1969, it became the album's second single, though it reached only 97 in the US.

This rendition has a string drone running towards the end – an idea from Melcher, who ran it through a phaser in a way similar to the drone on 'If You're Gone' on *Turn! Turn! Turn!*. If you listen closely, you can hear it, just. Another Melcher idea was to make it more of a pop record, as the band were doing a gospel version in concert, with each section built up through the addition of an extra voice. Though taken from a secular perspective, it manages to stay on the acceptable side of gospel-influenced rock, and avoids Christian-rock parody, though the instrumental middle section comes mighty close, saved by White's glorious guitar run.

The Doobie Brothers had a hit with a similar arrangement of the song in the early-1970s.

'It's All Over Now, Baby Blue' (Dylan)

This isn't a patch on the band's sparkly 1965 attempt, and is far too lethargic. In fact, it predates The Eagles California rock sound. The slow tempo – though closer to Dylan's original – just doesn't work, as The Byrds' best Dylan covers used to galvanize the songs. This bluesy take – suggested by Melcher – is lazy and listless. Melcher added some harmonies, and even put White's guitar through a Leslie speaker, but they both fail to enliven proceedings enough to avoid this sounding like routine filler. John York never liked this version, feeling Melcher pushed him out: he was pushed out to make way for Melcher's own harmonies.

White's bent guitar notes and McGuinn's world-weary vocal work well here, but the *Turn! Turn! Turn!* outtake is the best version. This new version is like the spirit of the 1960s fading away!

'There Must be Someone (I Can Turn To)' (Gosdin, Gosdin, Gosdin)

This was mainly written by Vern Gosdin of the Gosdin Brothers after his wife and kids left him. Parsons and White had both played on the Gosdin Brothers' version (which was originally a B-side).

McGuinn doesn't appear on this at all, but agreed to its inclusion as he was open to new ideas. It could do with one of his old 12-string runs. Even White's solo is a bit desultory, though the guitar lick near the end almost saves things. But generally, this doesn't sound like The Byrds at all.

'Gunga Din' (Parsons)

This is the album highlight, with the lovely fingerpicking and a double-tracked vocal from Gene Parsons. He was struggling with the open-D guitar tuning, and engineers were getting tetchy about the time being taken. But Clarence White demanded Parsons got sufficient time to cut the track, and it worked perfectly in the end. Parsons plays a lot of the instruments on this, but especially excels with his exquisite guitar-playing.

This is Gene Parsons' best Byrds composition, where the words 'Gunga Din' are only used to make up the rhyme. It was written partly about John York and his mother being refused entry to a restaurant because he wasn't wearing a jacket. It's also about a tour they were on where Chuck Berry didn't turn up for a gig. Berry was notorious for not playing if his payment wasn't received, so maybe this was the reason.

Close in spirit to the title track, it's simultaneously mournful and uplifting. The lovely repeating acoustic pattern really makes it great, and the subtle organ is also classy. This should've been a single, but a Byrds song with little McGuinn involvement was probably not going to be a single yet!

'Deportee (Plane Wreck at Los Gatos)' (Guthrie, Hoffman)

Following on from *Sweetheart*'s 'Pretty Boy Floyd', this Woody Guthrie cover about migrant fruit pickers lost in an air crash, works well. McGuinn had arranged a version for Judy Collins' *3* album, and thanks largely to the uplifting and languid instrumental break here, McGuinn avoids things getting too maudlin. He sings it with a certain knowing sadness, juxtaposed against Parsons' almost jolly drum pattern. It's a poignant homage to Guthrie. Surprisingly, McGuinn hasn't included it in his Folk Den project yet.

While it represents the band working as a tight unit, I agree with Johnny Rogan, in that, on its own, it works well, but as part of the album, it's questionable, given the number of covers.

'Armstrong, Aldrin and Collins' (Manners, Seely)

Here's a piece of genuine space rock, and one of the band's best closing tracks. (Not a huge amount of competition, admittedly.) This timely doff of the cap to the moon landing that year, doesn't outstay its welcome, and works as a quirky, cosmic, country meditation. The Byrds admitted it was their attempt at a 'We'll Meet Again' album ending, though the Zeke Manners song was originally very long, so they cut it down – a wise decision, as the other hymnlike Moog tracks in the Byrds canon tend to go on too long. But here, the song is dominated by McGuinn's earnest vocal as much as the Moog backing.

The lyric isn't solely about technology but divine intervention, and McGuinn became more immersed in Godliness in his solo career, as he did with the theme of folk and technology merging.

Connected Flights
'Way Behind the Sun' (Trad: arranged by McGuinn)
A modest but gorgeous rendition, John York suggested this, as he knew it from Pentangle's eponymous debut album. It should've been on *Ballad of Easy Rider*, as it's better than some of the album's other covers ('There Must be Someone') and the vocal is better than York's other one ('Fido'). The vocal is really effective, and – as usual – White's stellar laid-back picking is top-notch.

'Mae Jean Goes to Hollywood' (Browne)
This was written by the then-unknown songwriter Jackson Browne, and is a fairly nondescript bluegrass rendition.

'Fiddler a Dram (Moog Experiment)' (Trad: arranged by McGuinn)
Another folky Moog raga, this is McGuinn's attempt at making futuristic synth folk from an Appalachian dance melody. Though undeniably whimsical, it's an enjoyable experiment and probably would've ended the album in a decent quirky mode if they hadn't discovered 'Armstrong, Aldrin and Collins'. The vocal is playful, and the instrumental backing – with banjo and Moog – is sincere.

'Build it Up' (White, Parsons)
This instrumental would've been more than worthy of inclusion at the expense of 'It's All Over Now, Baby Blue'. Its Bakersfield sound could've been a tempo variation for the mournful side two. A catchy outtake, it showcases more of White's superb bluegrass picking, and Parsons' drumming is subtle enough to never impose on White's wonderful playing.

Note that this track only lasts for two and a half minutes – which is all you need, really. The CD reissue version includes a radio ad for the album.

'The Water is Wide' (Arrangement by The Byrds)
This appeared on the 2015 live *Lee Jeans Rock Concert 1969* CD. It's an unremarkable live run-through of a song McGuinn probably knew from his days playing the folk circuit. The sound quality isn't great, and the only interesting thing is White's guitar break.

Afterword
The album is well-sequenced, the band are tight, and it's more cohesive than the previous LP. While there are good songs, the songs McGuinn doesn't sing don't necessarily sound like The Byrds anymore. As Fonda's sleeve notes said,

The Byrds were 'lots of things'. Another unexpected thing they were about to become, was solid. For three years, the McGuinn/White/Parsons/Battin lineup was the band's most stable, and they were now such a hot live attraction that a double album (one live and one studio) was being considered.

(Untitled) (1970)

Personnel:
Roger McGuinn: 12-string guitar, synthesizer, vocals
Skip Battin: bass, vocals
Clarence White: guitars, mandolin, vocals
Gene Parsons: drums, guitars, harmonica, vocals
Byron Berline: fiddle
Sneaky Pete Kleinow: pedal steel
Producers: Terry Melcher, Jim Dickson
Record label: Columbia, CBS (UK)
Release date: 14 September 1970
Chart position: UK: 11, US: 40
Running time: 71:27

In John York's view, the band should've been breaking new ground to take full advantage of the new members' strengths, and he was fed up with singing and taking applause for songs made famous by other people. However, with his replacement Skip Battin in tow, this post-*Easy Rider* version of the band toured consistently until 1972, and was regarded as the best live Byrds lineup.

Though the album's working title was *Phoenix,* the eventual title happened by accident. Melcher had handwritten the word 'untitled' in the album title heading column, meaning it hadn't been given a title yet. But due to a secretarial blunder, the album was given the title *(Untitled),* and since the covers had already been printed, they just went with it.

Before the release of *(Untitled)* and Dylan's next album *Self Portrait,* rumours had circulated about the possibility of a Dylan/Byrds collaboration album, but it never went beyond the discussion stage. Instead, producers Terry Melcher and the returning Jim Dickson suggested the band release a double album of one live disc and one studio. It was hoped that revisiting some of their classics might provide a contrast between the sound of the original group and the current lineup.

The album sequencing was odd in that the live material was used on sides one and two. McGuinn wanted the studio album first but lost to Melcher, who insisted the live album come first.

The live half – culled from the early-1970 Queens College and Felt Forum performances – included new material and renditions of previous hit singles. The studio recordings mostly consisted of original material, including songs by McGuinn and friend Jacques Levy for a planned country-rock musical titled *Gene Tryp.* The musical was eventually abandoned, and many of the songs appeared on this and subsequent Byrds albums. The songs had nice *Workingman's Dead/American Beauty* Grateful Dead vibes, and represented a continued immersion in what became Americana.

The live recordings have gained a level of gravitas since the album's release, and the McGuinn/White duelling works best on side one of the live record.

But overall, it's an uneven album, with the live half – where they display admirable musicianship – probably preferable, though it sounds like you had to be there for some of it!

Though the studio set has its highlights, it's patchy, and somewhat overrated. Many saw *(Untitled)* as a return to form after *Ballad of Easy Rider*, but unfortunately, it's where the wheels start to come off the bus – and sadly, they would never really be fixed. The harmonies are faint or totally absent at times, and it's where the band's trajectory changes in terms of personal dynamics. Perhaps McGuinn became too aware of his reputation as a hirer/firer, and pushed the band too much as a creative democracy. This became apparent based on the non-McGuinn/Levy material, some of which lacked coherence.

(Untitled) gained decent reviews and sales. The band's commercial appeal had taken an upturn, thanks to their songs on *Easy Rider*. But more than that, their concerts regained their popularity. Though the album stalled at 40 in the US, it reached 11 in the UK, continuing the upward trend in popularity.

Melody Maker said The Byrds are one of the few bands whose music has the power to evoke nostalgia, and at the same time, make music which is completely representative of the present too. *Rolling Stone* was more lukewarm, saying that while it was hard to find fault with the album, it was still harder for diehard Byrd fans to be enthusiastic.

The album cover is not all that it seems. The staircase seems to rise from the Arizona landscape of Monument Valley, but it's actually at the Griffith Observatory in Los Angeles' Griffith Park, a desert scene replacing the original L.A. view. When the gatefold sleeve is opened, the front and back cover photographs are symmetrical, while the inside gatefold has more-moody black-and-white shots of the band looking much less hippie-ish than on the front cover.

Overall this was a harder – and at times more jazz-like – Byrds. Though bluegrass threads run through the album, it wasn't really country but more a harder-edged folk rock. In fact, at times they sounded like a rock band, especially on the live set.

The irony was that although they were now closer to a democracy than a dictatorship, McGuinn's songs here were the best. In the past, they'd needed conflict to ignite creativity, but the rest of the new band were no Clark, Crosby or Hillman when it came to songwriting.

One of the studio songs, 'Chestnut Mare', dwarfed everything else on the album – a song mainly written by McGuinn: still the leader in everyone's eyes.

Live Album

Generally, there won't be too much discussion about the tracks already covered under the studio albums.

'Lover of the Bayou' (McGuinn, Levy)

Things start with swamp rock, and the song the band were now opening most of their concerts with. One of the songs originally earmarked for the ill-fated *Gene Tryp* musical, its bayou references make it sound like a cross between Dr. John and Creedence Clearwater Revival.

White's guitar rips along, and the band do sound psychic here – belying a group who had a reputation for being an average live band in their earlier incarnations. McGuinn's raspy vocals weren't supposed to be sung in the character of Gene Tryp, but in that of a voodoo witch doctor called Big Cat.

A studio version of this would've been nice, as it could've enhanced one of the next two studio albums. However, an unreleased studio version is discussed in the Connected Flights section of this chapter, and also, a more-soulful unreleased live take from Queens College was released in the 1990 box set.

'Positively 4th Street' (Dylan)
This is a decent live song that they never recorded in the studio. White's guitar drives the song, with the string bender sounding like a pedal steel.

Though the song was now five years old, maybe McGuinn thought the caustic lyric suited this turbulent time in the band's career – in terms of music critics and radio stations having indifferent reactions to the band's recent work. Or maybe it was a dig at Dylan, as there were rumours the two had fallen out, hence the speculated Dylan/Byrds studio album never getting off the ground. McGuinn sings with lots of gravitas, but his hoarse vocal was the result of too much cocaine.

This was the last Dylan song on a Byrds record until the 1990 reunion sessions.

'Nashville West' (Parsons, White)
This is a pleasant-enough run-through, though Gene Parsons felt the *Dr. Byrds* version was better. (But bear in mind that he already thought the old Nashville West version was better than the *Dr. Byrds* version.)

'So You Want to Be a Rock 'N' Roll Star' (McGuinn, Hillman)
This likeable version has a similar tempo to the studio gem, but with a beefier arrangement. White and McGuinn's guitar interplay is a joy, and Parsons' drumming adds an early-1970s drive without ever being overbearing. But McGuinn's gravelly cocaine voice may grate on some listeners, and he seems to struggle with his diction slightly in the last verse.

'Mr. Tambourine Man' (Dylan)
'Mr. Spaceman' (McGuinn)
These come across as crowd pleasers and offer nothing new: not even White's solo on 'Mr. Spaceman'. And the former is really quite a tired run-through.

'Eight Miles High' (McGuinn, Crosby, Clark)
This is the ultimate combination of old Byrds meeting new Byrds. Though it stemmed from a live medley (with 'Mr. Tambourine Man' and 'Turn! Turn! Turn!'), they now performed the song on its own.

It's a highlight for some fans, and showcases that particular band's improvisation skills. They speak to each other in a language that few – if any – earlier Byrds lineups ever did in concert. McGuinn's guitar work shines as much as White's here – their improvised conversation (which thankfully avoids any self-indulgent guitar-virtuoso posturing) is quite wonderful in places, reinventing the song as a raga country-rock jam. The Byrds weren't jammers, but now that White had joined, they could intensify the guitar arrangements.

However, the drum and bass solos are just too much. Their meandering noodling feels hours long – so much so that it takes up all of side two – and it takes too long for the familiar vocals to appear.

After 'Eight Miles High' there's an unlisted version of the stage favourite 'Hold It', previously heard at the end of the closing medley on *Dr. Byrds*.

Studio Album
'Chestnut Mare' (McGuinn, Levy)

As The Byrds' best song of the 1970s, an edited version gave them their first UK top-20 hit since 1965. With its serene McGuinn/White guitar combination and its glorious euphoric chorus, it harks back to past glories. McGuinn wrote most of the music on a cliff in Santa Domingo seven years earlier, during a Chad Mitchell Trio tour. Jacques Levy wrote the rest of it for inclusion in *Gene Tryp*, where the lyric changes *Peer Gynt's* reindeer being chased, into attempting to tame a wild horse, and it becomes an old-time cowboy story about America.

McGuinn turns in one of his finest vocal performances here – his only criticism being that he felt that he didn't sing the long note at the end very well. With rich vocals set against the blend of acoustic and electric guitars, the pleasant, airy sound represented the closest to the old Byrds sound in over two years: thus, many journalists called it an instant Byrds classic. Writing for *Fusion*, Ben Edmonds referred to wings healing, and cast those fans who'd abandoned the ship too soon as 'guilty'.

The idea of a partly-spoken song about a horse might sound gauche (and the talking might kill the pace a little bit), but the spoken part adds drama with its *Gene Tryp* theatrical context. Of course, the irresistible chorus is the real hook, and there's a real feeling of the band again attempting something transcendent and lasting. The last chorus – with its 'I'm going to catch that horse if I can' line and McGuinn's higher melody variations – is blissful and the peak of this Byrds incarnation. It felt as if briefly they were using their 1960s past to create a new sound for the new decade.

Incredibly, the US single only reached 121, but the fact it used the unedited album version might explain it. The UK single edited out the second verse and middle section.

This ethereal time-travelling cowboy opus became McGuinn's late-period Byrds signature tune, and was an FM-radio favourite in the 1970s. It's also a song that Dylan asked McGuinn to include on the 1975/1976 *Rolling Thunder Revue* tour.

If only the rest of the studio album had songs of this standard.

'Truck Stop Girl' (George, Payne)

This is a cover of a Little Feat song, who were still unknown to the public at this stage. White knew Lowell George from the studio where both bands recorded. Sadly, this song about a tragic road death – sung by White with a quiet vigour – took on more poignancy a few years later when White died in a hit-and-run accident. The Byrds version is almost a White solo effort, with the pathos in his vocals suggesting nothing unseemly.

It's a perfectly decent – if unspectacular – version, where White's closing guitar break suggests McGuinn must've been busy with *Gene Tryp*, as he's hardly involved here at all. The lack of harmonies also highlights the fact they're not trying anything too different here, and the track probably lacks McGuinn's creative guidance.

Little Feat's version – which appeared in early-1971 – is stronger. But it's a testament to The Byrds' taste that they could source material from an unknown band who were about to become one of the best bands of the 1970s.

'All the Things' (McGuinn, Levy)

This *Gene Tryp* McGuinn song of disillusionment is an album highlight and includes Gram Parsons on backing vocals and producer Terry Melcher on piano. Parsons and McGuinn were regularly hanging out together again, but Melcher admits to being drunk when he agreed to Parsons appearing on the track.

This is one of McGuinn's better late-period Byrds songs. He sings it with worldly-wise experience, and it's one of his first to refer to God and the universe.

The longer alternative CD reissue version is better – McGuinn's vocal is more up-front, and the guitar break works better than the standard middle-eight in the album version. The guitar part is generally more Byrdsian, and the hummed harmonies at the end are glorious.

Check out the great version by Miracle Legion as a bonus track on the 1989 *Time Between* Byrds tribute album, also featuring Dinosaur Jnr., Thin White Rope and Giant Sand.

'Yesterday's Train' (Parsons, Battin)

This gentle folk/country ballad about reincarnation was inspired by Skip Battin's involvement with Buddhism. With Gene Parsons on lead vocals and harmonica, Burrito Brother Sneaky Pete Kleinow plays steel guitar, and the musicianship is admirable. But the track highlight – the middle eight and instrumental passage towards the end – should've been developed instead of just fading out, which is an unsatisfactory ending. A more-lean unplugged version appears on the CD reissue.

A spoiler alert for the rest of the book – although I like this track, I have never been a fan of Skip Battin's songs, which take a more dominant role from around the time of *(Untitled)*.

'Hungry Planet' (Battin, Fowley, McGuinn)

This was the first song the band recorded by Skip Battin and Kim Fowley. McGuinn also has a credit here, as he restructured the melody, though it is a bit clumsy. The song has a decent riff, but it goes on too long without going anywhere, and even Battin later admitted that none of the band particularly liked the way it came out.

The middle eight doesn't enhance the song, and the track sounds like a work in progress, though the little acoustic guitar lick almost saves it. Moreover, McGuinn sings with little conviction, which makes you wonder why the track was used.

'Just a Season' (McGuinn, Levy)

This great track is another of the 25 McGuinn/Levy *Gene Tryp* songs. While Clark's songs might've overshadowed McGuinn's in the original Byrds (later matched by Crosby and Hillman), McGuinn was now clearly the band's strongest writer, especially when on his A-game like this.

There's a tender, melancholy Laurel Canyon groove throughout, especially with the chorus harmonies and instrumental break. It also has one of McGuinn's finest lyrics – the profound and intimate 'circles without reason' phrase is the *Gene Tryp* character looking for his lost love. The themes of reincarnation and the journey of life take on more poignancy with the line, 'It really wasn't hard to be a star', echoing The Byrds' immediate success but now living with less commercial fortune.

This – like all the McGuinn/Levy songs on here – earned *(Untitled)* a positive reputation. An earlier alternate take appears on the 1990 box set. Interestingly, Terry Melcher covered this on his eponymous 1974 album, with Hillman and Clarke appearing.

'Take a Whiff on Me' (Ledbetter, Lomax, Lomax)

The Byrds' tribute to Leadbelly was originally titled 'Cocaine Habit Blues' and was intended for the *Ballad of Easy Rider* LP. At Jim Dickson's suggestion, White took the lead vocal here, but the track's country style doesn't really work, and the tongue-in-cheek tone grates after a few verses.

White's supreme bluegrass picking and mandolin overdubs are admirable, but his nasal vocal makes the words difficult to decipher at times, and McGuinn would've probably sung it better. Parsons' drumming tries to drive the track, but it's just an uninspired cover version, especially the pedestrian instrumental break. McGuinn later joked that there were too many whiffs on this!

'You All Look Alike' (Battin, Fowley)

This sarcastic generation-gap variation on the murder ballad – with a dead longhair mourned in the chorus – features Byron Berline on eerie fiddle: a highlight on an otherwise average track. McGuinn's lead vocal fails to save the track from being album filler, especially when compared to his excellent contributions to this album. White's mandolin is also a delight, but it's too quiet, and could have given the track more impetus if it was louder.

Kim Fowley's Byrds co-writes generally aren't very good. He'd be better remembered for his liner notes to the 1973 *History of the Byrds* compilation, where he praised the early Byrds and used good reference points such as Dylan's comment about the Byrds being able to do things which most people don't know about.

As for the song, it's dull and inconsequential.

'Well Come Back Home' (Battin)

This tedious Battin song was originally titled 'Welcome Back Home'. The anti-Vietnam sentiment is understandable, and it's heartfelt enough, probably owing to Battin having a friend who died in the conflict. But the song is too long, and the chant – inspired by Battin's initiation into Buddhism – sounds forced. McGuinn provides a wonky raga-like groove, but the chants ultimately dominate. The chant 'Nam myoho renge kyo' is meant to be the highest sound in the universe: not that you can tell from this weary rendition.

Some reissues wrongly refer to the song as 'Welcome Back Home'.

Connected Flights
'Lover of the Bayou' (McGuinn, Levy)

This studio version of the live favourite appeared on the CD reissue. Another song written for *Gene Tryp*, it could have sat comfortably on *Byrdmaniax* or *Farther Along,* but maybe it should've been on *this* album, as it could've been a side opener for both the live and studio albums. Sadly, the song seems to have been forgotten about after they had trouble raising funds for the *Gene Tryp* production.

The instrumental passage works really well – a lovely contrast between wistful harmonica and improvised Rickenbacker. The only downside is the piercing harmonica part at the beginning, and McGuinn's echoey vocals now sound dated, but it's an outtake that was more than worthy of gracing any 1970s Byrds album.

'Kathleen's Song' (McGuinn, Levy)

This song is covered in the next chapter, but this is a wonderful version, and much better without the orchestration of the *Byrdmaniax* version.

This version was originally released in the 1990 box set, and appears on the CD reissue. It should've been on *(Untitled)*, certainly in place of one of the Battin/Fowley songs.

'White's Lightning' (White, McGuinn)

This studio jam, unreleased until the 1990 box set, has never appeared on any *(Untitled)* reissue. It was recorded in June 1970, and logged in the CBS files as 'Fifteen Minute Jam'. It's probably for Byrds completists only.

'White's Lightning Pt.2' (McGuinn, White)

This is a different edit of the same jam, though it's probably still too long, even allowing for the great Clarence. But it's an interesting-enough Byrds artefact, and it's easy to imagine them playing this at soundchecks. Far from being a White signature tune, this was understandably left off the album, and only appeared on the *(Untitled)* CD reissue.

'Willin'' (George)

This Little Feat cover was sung by Parsons. Maybe they felt that one Lowell George song was enough, but this could've replaced one of the Battin/Fowley filler songs. It's a respectful version, but lacks the gravitas of Lowell George's vocal on the Little Feat version, and is probably mainly for Byrds fanatics.

Byrdfact: the CD reissue version is a different mix to the live version on 1990's *The Byrds* box set.

'It's Alright Ma (I'm Only Bleeding)' (Dylan)

Similar to McGuinn's *Easy Rider* version, the harmonica flourishes are a bit much here. It's difficult to see why anybody would be interested in this version of what was a five-year-old Dylan song. It's respectable, but it's perfectly understandable why it was left off the original album.

It's from a Felt Forum concert, and appears on the *(Untitled)* CD reissue. The rest of the concert's tracks have appeared elsewhere and generally add nothing to the originals.

'Black Mountain Rag (Soldier's Joy)' (Berline: arranged by White, McGuinn)

Originally on the 1990 box set, this was an acoustic interlude from Queen's College in New York on the same night as the 'Lover of the Bayou' take in the box set. It was a live favourite in the early-1970s, highlighted by White's great bluegrass pickin'.

Another version appears on *Straight For The Sun* – a 1971 live set released in 2014 – where it's part of a medley with 'Mr. Tambourine Man'.

(Album coda)
'Amazing Grace' (Newton)

Though they were originally going to cut 'Onward Christian Soldiers', they chose an *a cappella* version of 'Amazing Grace' as an album coda. The idea was scrapped, but it was included uncredited at the end of the CD reissue after the Felt Form version of 'This Wheel's On Fire'. It's perfectly well-sung, and though not a huge loss to the album, it's nice to hear.

Afterword

(Untitled) was a good album but contained some uninspired choices. Maybe The Byrds were content to be a great working live band, and, after all, McGuinn claimed they were still successful financially, and he reckoned this lineup was a better *live* act, while the original Byrds were better in the studio.

Ominously, McGuinn played the *(Untitled)* tapes to members of the old Byrds, and they liked it. As such, the band explored songs in a similar style, and looked to expand on Battin's funky bass lines. This was to inform the next album, along with Terry Melcher's idea to add more strings. What could possibly go wrong??

Byrdmaniax (1971)

Personnel:
Roger McGuinn: 12-string guitar, vocals
Skip Battin: bass, vocals
Clarence White: guitars, mandolin, vocals
Gene Parsons: drums, harmonica, banjo, vocals
Larry Knechtel: piano, organ
Sneaky Pete Kleinow: pedal steel
Byron Berline: fiddle
Jimmi Seiter: percussion
Producers: Terry Melcher, Chris Hinshaw
Record label: Columbia, CBS (UK)
Release date: 23 June 1971
Chart position: UK: -, US: 46
Running time: 34:06

The group's enthusiastic concert responses were a hopeful sign, but over the next two albums, they rarely prioritised melody. Unfortunately, much of the new album was half-baked and underdeveloped writing-wise and eventually over-baked and over-developed production-wise. After the sessions (while they were touring) Melcher mixed the album without the band knowing. He also overdubbed strings, horns and a gospel choir onto many of the songs – generally giving the album a messy, overproduced feel, and at times a really gloomy sound.

Drummer Gene Parsons said the band wanted the orchestration removed and the album remixed, but Columbia Records refused as the project was already over budget. Parsons coined the phrase 'Melcher's folly', and did a good job underselling it, complaining that Melcher and engineer Chris Hinshaw made what was *their* idea of a Byrds album. White later echoed Parsons' feelings. Melcher's folly reportedly cost a staggering $100,000! Before its release, McGuinn joked about calling the album *Expensive!*.

McGuinn once said he never wanted to be labelled, never wanted the Byrds to be called country rock, folk rock or raga rock. Perhaps that was the album's problem; it just didn't know what it was. Most reviewers agreed that Melcher's orchestrations ruined *Byrdmaniax* and made it devoid of any signature Byrds sound. But Melcher's counterargument that the performances were lacklustre, also has merit – especially the Battin/Fowley songs, which make little use of White's talent or any traditional Byrds strengths. In truth, Melcher probably gets overly criticised for this lumpish effort, as the songs *were* generally weak and had an overbalance of pastiche. But that doesn't excuse the predominant mushy overdubs.

Though the press were unanimous in their praise of The Byrds' concerts at this time, they were also virtually unanimous in their critical mauling of the album. *Rolling Stone* described The Byrds as a boring dead group, and scathingly dismissed the album as 'increments of pus', suggesting the overdubs were preposterous in places.

Initially, McGuinn was contrary, scathingly telling M*elody Maker* in 1971: 'The present Byrds are better than the old Byrds by 97.6%.' But he was clearly being defensive, and later blamed Melcher for the outcome of the album, saying he hated it. The *NME* agreed, saying the orchestration was all very well for some bands but not on this showing for The Byrds. Remarkably, *Melody Maker* gave a good review, saying the album stood on its own without need for comparison, adding that it was ridiculously varied and what they expected from the best rock-'n'-roll band this side of 1984!?!?

McGuinn later conceded that though the overdubs were not to his taste, he shouldn't have said it was the producer's ideas, as it wasn't professional or good for promotion, but that was how he felt. His concerns were probably fuelled by his worries that by 1971 they weren't making 'as much bread' either.

The cover image of the four in silver death masks was dreadful. Designers from Columbia's art department actually designed the masks, and an artist actually created them! They mirrored much of the music, as they can be seen as lifeless metaphors for the album.

Most fans now regard the album as the band's worst: their creative nadir. On the tour to promote the album, roadie Jimmi Seiter played extra percussion, but he left the band in late-1971.

'Glory, Glory' (Reynolds)

Lord, this poor opening track (suggested by Gene Parsons) is hammy hippie gospel. Merry Clayton sings backing vocals, and Larry Knechtel plays piano on this version of the song. But it's fairly listless, sounding like a hippie take of a hymn like 'Oh Happy Day'. It just doesn't work in the way that 'Jesus is Just Alright' worked. There's also a shade of the dreadful 'Lay Lady Lay' chorus here, and no amount of Clayton backing vocals can save it.

This was released as a single, but didn't chart, unsurprisingly. And maybe it was apt that it was the album opener, since the overdubs represent a microcosm of the whole album.

'Pale Blue' (McGuinn, Parsons)

This is one of the album's strongest tracks, though that's not necessarily something to boast about. In fairness, the orchestration is Melcher's biggest success here – it's not too gauche, and adds some pathos. The harmonica breaks work well too. It's one of the few tracks where Melcher's *Ballad of Easy Rider* production influence, works. The violins aren't overdone – in fact, they highlight Melcher's intuitive arranging gift. The criticism of his work on *Byrdmaniax* isn't that he used *strings*, but that he used too many. But on this song about longing, he gets it right by achieving just the right amount of melancholy.

The song also shows that McGuinn was a very good balladeer. Strangely, they didn't play it live very often. McGuinn sings it well on record, so maybe his hoarse concert voice just didn't work for this song.

Melcher felt that the contrast of harmonica and strings was the closest he got to the sound he wanted for the album. Even so, the CD-reissue version, minus overdubs, works better, as do most of the unreleased un-orchestrated tracks.

'I Trust (Everything is Gonna Work out Alright)' (McGuinn)

Had this been the opening track, it would've made the album more uneven and front-loaded, as this and 'Pale Blue' are the best tracks here. Again, McGuinn was providing the best – in fact, maybe the only decent – original material.

You can still hear his Rickenbacker on the chorus (albeit almost drowned-out by the piano), and it's one of their better, less-mawkish attempts at gospel, like a sweet spiritual with Americana pedal steel. It's a McGuinn signature song – lyrically at least, as the title and sub-title is a phrase he often used if others were going through a bad time or had concerns about the band's fortunes. Billy James had also quoted the phrase as early as the band's first album liner notes. McGuinn originally borrowed the phrase from the Norman Vincent Peale book *The Power of Positive Thinking*.

The song's bland optimism works. Save for another overproduction, the gospel backing works better here, though the track could've used some signature Rickenbacker over the verses. Unlike the original Byrds, McGuinn was the only current member who seemed able to write introspective lyrics (apart from Battin's Buddhist songs), which were something that could've enhanced the album. Strangely, compared to some of the preening self-indulgence of the then-growing early-1970s singer-songwriter movement, this track has maybe aged better than other songs of self-contemplation from the era.

Byrdfact: they apparently appeared on *Top of the Pops* to promote this, but it failed to influence sales. (The footage is presumably long since lost.)

'Tunnel of Love' (Battin, Fowley)

All the organ and saxophone can't save this 1950s novelty tribute to 'Blueberry Hill'. It's terrible musically, and – ironically – the theme of the writer remembering better days was an accidentally accurate metaphor for the band's current status.

It has a bit of an R&B, Delaney & Bonnie influence, but it's really weak and perfunctory. It sounds like a Skip Battin solo track, and even Gene Parsons admitted that they recorded songs like this due to a dearth of material.

'Citizen Kane' (Battin, Fowley)

This hopeless homage to old Hollywood was unsurprisingly written very quickly. The Melcher trad-jazz overdub is, frankly, embarrassing. This early into the album, the pastiche is already wearing thin. Battin would later include this piece of whimsy on his *Navigator* solo album, though this could be because his weary, gravelly vocal does suit the subject matter.

'I Wanna Grow Up to Be a Politician' (McGuinn, Levy)

This novelty throwaway was written for *Gene Tryp*, where the main character was running for president. Though set in the 19th century, the satirical elements were apt for the cynicism of the Nixon era.

This is the sort of sardonic song that Randy Newman can write in his sleep. But in the hands of this Byrds lineup, it sounds too flimsy. Musically – though the band (certainly McGuinn) were intrinsically drawn to new sounds – the law of diminishing returns continued with this lame duck. It's a clumsy and toothless satire, and the vaudeville brass band adds nothing. It's hard to see how something so jaunty would ever resonate with fans of protest music – especially in the early-1970s when listeners were used to the more-virtuous readings of the burgeoning singer-songwriter movement.

'Absolute Happiness' (Battin, Fowley)

This song about the search for contentment was presumably inspired by Battin's immersion in Buddhism. It works slightly better than the other Battin/Fowley songs, probably because Melcher's influence is felt the least. The instrumental break almost saves the song, especially with the subtle organ runs. Fowley later disagreed with Battin that this was about Buddhism. He said it was about a guru with a religious hideaway in Hawaii.

'Green Apple Quick Step' (Parsons, White)

Parsons and White here show off old-time country chops; the bluegrass mandolin providing a spark of up-tempo life. Melcher tried to overdub three Byron Berline fiddle parts, but it proved impossible. Berline (who felt isolated during the recording) and Gene Parsons were not impressed with Melcher's intervention, though they denied rumours that the tapes were sped-up for effect.

Though the band never quite liked it, the track is an album highlight. Without turning it into a bluegrass album, they could've added a few more tracks of this exuberant nature, to help vary the tempo at the very least.

'My Destiny' (Carter)

Prior to the album's release, McGuinn said this would be the album's only country song: 'a super country song with steel guitar'. White sings the lead vocal here. It's a song he first heard in his earlier bluegrass days, and it does highlight the album's eclecticism, even if it doesn't work that well.

Sneaky Pete Kleinow's pedal steel-playing is the highlight, while White's moving vocal works quite well, albeit losing its vulnerability thanks to the overly-nasal vocal. Mind you, the vocals certainly work much better than the Floyd Cramer piano style.

Overall, the humdrum musical backing (apart from Kleinow) makes it dirge-like album filler.

'Kathleen's Song' (McGuinn, Levy)

This was the last *Gene Tryp* song that The Byrds recorded, and was even listed on the original run of *(Untitled)* album covers before it was removed from the track list due to a 'lack of space'. But it would've been a better option than some of the tracks that did appear.

Again, it highlights the prominent overdubs, but it is a good song. Though the strings don't necessarily enhance it, it's a charming piece of orchestrated pop that teases what the album could've been like. Tellingly, when McGuinn heard the orchestra recording their part, he assumed he'd gone into the wrong studio, as he didn't recognise his own song.

'Jamaica Say You Will' (Browne)

While this is some fans' favourite song on the album, the band didn't like it much, as White had apparently cut a far better vocal version. Though the 40-piece orchestra drowned out what was actually a decent song, the track's appealing traits are like a trip down Byrds memory lane. McGuinn's distinctive guitar work and the vocal harmonies try to save the day, but both are too rare on the album, and all the vocals are buried in the mix. It wasn't a particularly inspired take. Even minus overdubs, it would've sounded lacklustre.

Intriguingly, Battin, White, Parsons and Browne (on piano) cut a better version, but it remains unreleased. After the Kentucky Colonels, White had never wanted to sing again until he heard Browne's songs. Poignantly, he also thought that it would influence him into more writing.

Connected Flights
'Just Like a Woman' (Dylan)

This thin country-gospel outtake was included on the CD reissue. They originally tried a version for *(Untitled)*, though it would've been great to hear the original Byrds cover this.

This is a rather tepid attempt, though the organ is pleasant enough, but it doesn't bear comparison with Bob's 'thin wild mercury' sound. The band might've realised the lack of imagination here themselves, as it was the last Dylan song they recorded until 'Paths of Victory' on the 1990 box set.

'Think I'm Gonna Feel Better' (Clark)

This was originally on the *Gene Clark with The Gosdin Brothers* album. White played on that, and remembered it fondly enough to attempt this version for *Byrdmaniax*. But it's a bit of a mess, and while they would've taken more time if they'd seriously considered it for album inclusion, it's out of tune, and White's vocal isn't convincing at all.

'Byrdgrass' (Parsons, White)

An interesting curio at the end of the CD reissue, this includes some studio chatter featuring Clarence White's father, Eric. Musically it's just an early harmonica-laden take of 'Green Apple Quick Step'.

'Nothin' to It' (Watson)

This is a decent run-through of the bluegrass instrumental made famous by Doc Watson. It appears on the 1971 soundtrack of the *Earl Scruggs Performing With His Family And Friends* TV special, on which The Byrds performed 'You Ain't Goin' Nowhere' with Scruggs.

Afterword

The worst Byrds' album! For a band that spent the 1960s as pioneers, this was a woefully disappointing record. They should have been challenging both Crosby, Stills, Nash & Young and The Eagles. But with this form, even bands like Poco sounded more cutting-edge.

Previously, band troubles had been a creative catalyst for freewheeling studio experimentation, but now the band's main focus was to record a quick follow-up to eradicate the disaster that was *Byrdmaniax*.

Farther Along (1971)

Personnel:
Roger McGuinn: 12-string guitar, vocals
Skip Battin: bass, piano, vocals
Clarence White: guitars, mandolin, vocals
Gene Parsons: drums, harmonica, banjo, guitar, pedal steel, vocals
Producer: The Byrds
Record label: Columbia, CBS (UK)
Release date: US: 17 November 1971, UK: January 1972
Chart position: UK: -, US: 152
Running time: 32:02

In July 1971 – incredibly only a month after the *Byrdmaniax* release, The Byrds began recording the follow-up, electing to produce it themselves. Though slightly better than its predecessor, the speed they recorded it, resulted in an album almost as flawed. The lack of preparation, mediocre songwriting and absence of a supervisor were all clear. It could've also been a reflection of the drugs now influencing the music scene. Speed wasn't feeding any manic urgency into recordings, nor was acid creating any head-spinning sonic landscapes. Cocaine was now the drug of choice, but that couldn't really be blamed, as that tended to result in self-indulgent subject matter or posturing virtuoso musicianship. Moreover, the material was just terribly stale and listless. Perhaps they needed the dynamic arguments of old. Those had sparked The Byrds' greatest achievements, and these later recordings needed a spark to avoid everything being so pedestrian and dull.

Melcher's production might've helped a few songs here. The album – originally to be called *Home Made* because they produced it themselves – still had a country-rock sound. It also paid homage to the rock-'n'-roll era. There's a half-decent album in there, but they desperately needed the objectivity of an outside producer to help root out the chaff.

In November 1971 – less than five months after the release of *Byrdmaniax* – The Byrds issued *Farther Along* (delayed until January 1972 in the UK). The reception garnered only slightly better reviews than *Byrdmaniax*. *Melody Maker* again gave positive feedback, saying it was good to hear The Byrds stretching their wings again. Robert Christgau was more scathing, suggesting they were 'farther along on a downhill road'. He thought *Byrdmaniax* was better than *Farther Along*, but complained that if you can only tell arithmetically, how much difference does it really make? Fair point, except *Farther Along,* is the better of the two, probably thanks to 'Bugler'.

Through the years, there have been more mixed feelings about the album. Sid Griffin suggests this is the point where the band became directionless, using the example of a roadie's involvement as evidence. McGuinn later admitted that nobody in the band really liked it, saying it was too eclectic – or worse, suggesting that maybe The Byrds had just lost their appeal. His later observation is probably correct: if the album was eclectic *but* decent, then more people would've bought it.

The cover showed a tired band looking like a bigger bunch of long-haired hippies than they did in the days when they influenced the emergent Sunset Strip counterculture. *Farther Along* certainly was no triumphant return, and McGuinn's influence was now missing too often. He'd clearly lost his songwriting chops, becoming too reliant on the mediocre material of others. Frankly, some of it was worse than mediocre. And was it now necessary to have all members take a lead vocal? Maybe McGuinn was now just too content with *Easy Rider* royalties and concert takings that he wasn't stimulated to write anymore.

Though the album is quite listenable in places, generally, it sounds tired – emblematic of a band running out of ideas and rush-releasing a follow-up. *Farther Along* ventured nowhere they hadn't been before, and was only slightly better than *Byrdmaniax*.

'Tiffany Queen' (McGuinn)

This has a promising power pop-opening, including the return of the trusted Rickenbacker arpeggios. But though you can hear what Big Star were listening to, it ultimately fails to fulfil its promise, and becomes a bit of a rock parody.

Written, rehearsed and recorded in one day, it's jovial but slight. Though there are echoes of 'Bob Dylan's 115th Dream' and Chuck Berry's 'Promised Land', it comes nowhere near the excitement of those two American classics. On tracks like this, McGuinn's slender voice is unconvincing without the celestial Byrdsian harmonies. Almost as unconvincing is the rock-'n'-roll guitar break, with a dash of Rickenbacker.

McGuinn later wrote 'Tiffany Queen II' for his current wife Camilla. The song has a tangled love-affair history. Apparently, McGuinn wrote the original 'Tiffany Queen' about his then-partner Linda Gilbert, who played with a Tiffany lamp at the house McGuinn still shared with his wife, Dolores. (She changed her name to Ianthe when McGuinn changed his middle name to Roger.) Apparently, Dolores still owns the same Tiffany lamp.

The most telling thing is that this song constitutes McGuinn's sole composition on the record. A lesson not learned from *Byrdmaniax*.

'Get Down Your Line' (Parsons)

The band could've applied this song's philosophy of self-improvement to their own output – this track could've been improved, except for the instrumental passage and the guitar run before it comes back to the chorus. While it is enlivened by a wailing harmonica, the harmonies are half-baked, and the drums are too loud. And while White's guitar work is sterling, the biggest problem is the vocal effect, which does little to enhance the arrangement. It's a limp country gallop that doesn't know where it's going. Also, the verse chords are very similar to those in the *(Untitled)* cut 'Yesterday's Train'.

'Farther Along' (Trad: arranged by White)

White sings the title track, with the rest of the band harmonising. Sadly, the song was White's epitaph when Gram Parsons and Bernie Leadon played it at his funeral in July 1973. It took on a double poignancy when Gram Parsons himself died two months later.

With its going-back-to-basics feel and multi-harmonies, it's assumed this was the band's revenge for 'Glory Glory' on the previous album. However, there's little involvement from McGuinn, and if the band were making a statement, surely he'd have been more involved.

This folky bluegrass take on a gospel hymn is a return to *Sweetheart* terrain, and is also similar to some of the Burrito's soulful arrangements. (They covered this on *Burrito Deluxe*.) Though the Burrito's version was probably the best-known at the time, White based his phrasing on the Rose Maddox version. But the Byrds version with White's soulful arrangement is better. He sings it with a pleasant conviction, with nice piano touches, banjo and mandolin.

'B.B. Class Road' (Parsons, Dawson)

The beer bottle sound effect was roadie and sound engineer Stuart 'Dinky' Dawson's idea. Yup – the band that created 'Eight Miles High' were now taking onboard boozy sound effects implemented by their roadie! And it's a million miles from the Firesign Theatre's ingenious sound effects on 'Draft Morning'. Parsons sings in the guise of a trucker, but it ends up sounding like a disposable roadie's song, which is basically what it is! For years it was assumed that Dawson sang this, but Parsons admitted to it years later, parodying the bar-brawl chaos of touring life and trucking. Straying the way of *Byrdmaniax* with its lighthearted feel and trudging attempt at a boogie arrangement, this is leftover filler, and more evidence of McGuinn's lack of interest in a creative sense. It's another unrecognisable Byrds track.

'Bugler' (Murray)

This is the album's best track, and was written by Larry Murray: Chris Hillman's former Scottsville Squirrel Barkers colleague. It represents the last – and best – of the dog song trilogy, started with 'Old Blue' and continued with 'Fido'.

Like the best parts of *Notorious*, there's a pining nostalgia, especially with White's vocals. It's a slightly overlooked late-period highlight, though admittedly, most Byrdmaniacs do love it – especially the gentle, rolling country-rock lilt. The chorus harmonies are gorgeous, and Parson's steel guitar is a great counterpoint to the vocals.

White claims he knew they were mixing the album quickly and poorly, and initially deliberately messed up his vocal. Keen to avoid the overdubbing fiasco that almost ruined 'Jamaica Say You Will' on *Byrdmaniax*, he returned to the studio to sort out this track, adding the beautiful mandolin run reminiscent of Rod Stewart's then-current hit 'Maggie Mae', which really enhances the texture.

Sadly, it's another track with added poignancy, as White tells the tale of a dog who died in a road accident: White's best Byrd vocal. More than any other, this track makes you wonder what they could've achieved on *Byrdmaniax* and *Farther Along* had they taken more time. This really should've been a single instead of the next track.

'America's Great National Pastime' (Battin, Fowley)

Talk about phoning in a performance: Battin and Fowley wrote this over the phone in 20 minutes. Byrds biographer Johnny Rogan referred to this as: 'The severest loss of musical identity the band has ever suffered'. More novelty nonsense, it's based on a Coca Cola ad. Incredibly it was released as a single in November 1971 but failed to chart anywhere. Battin's voice is awful, and the only listenable part is the instrumental passage. It's easy to see why this plodding, vaudeville throwaway never got any airplay in the early-1970s when Britain had glam and the US had the burgeoning FM radio. The lyric, too, is over the top with its overuse of puns about American life. The single was mercifully withdrawn shortly after release.

'Antique Sandy' (McGuinn, Battin, Parsons, White, Seiter)

All is not usually well when the roadie gets a writing credit. It's written about Seiter's flower-child girlfriend, who lived in the woods and collected antiques. With its muddy mix and grating vocal effects, it revisits *Byrdmaniax*. And while the harmonies might suggest they took time with this, they add nothing, and it's another lame offering. At least McGuinn took an interest by singing it. Also, the piano interlude is out of place – a languid McGuinn or gentle bluegrass White guitar break could've worked much better.

Seiter claims he has never earned any money from this.

'Precious Kate' (Fowley, Battin)

This is a love song about James Taylor's sister, sung by McGuinn. To be fair, he sings it brightly, and there's a teasing Rickenbacker guitar run throughout. Battin later admitted it was written 'in about 5 minutes'.

The backing track foresees the enigmatic work of the wonderful Wilco, with Battin's bass line predicting some of John Stirratt's bass work. But overall, it's like a mediocre outtake from *The Basement Tapes* at best, which is a shame because, had they spent more time on it, it could at least have had a more harmonious chorus. But like so much of this album, they recorded things too quickly, being hell-bent on eradicating the *Byrdmaniax* disaster.

'So Fine' (Otis)

Based on the rock-'n'-roll homages of The Beatles (on the *Get Back* sessions) and Creedence Clearwater Revival, returning to the 1950s to source or inform material was clearly hip in the late-1960s/early-1970s. But in The Byrds' case, a lack of creativity and songwriting chops were highlighted by this mediocre take on a frankly average song. Recorded by The Fiestas in 1959, this was White's idea. He liked the song in his youth – another example of McGuinn's reducing influence on song selection. There was a 1950s feel to the album generally. Perhaps their fondness for the music of their youth was a catalyst to feeling unified and relating to each other in these creatively trying times.

It does sport a brief flash of Byrdsian harmonies, but otherwise, it's dispensable. While the source material simply wasn't good enough in the first place, it reaches unsurpassed heights of humdrum in the lazy instrumental break, which cries out for a Gary Usher to arrange it into something better than this uninspired and rushed version.

'Lazy Waters' (Rafkin)
Some critics found Battin's singing too melodramatic, but this is his best vocal as a Byrd, by quite a distance. It's sung with feeling, and backed by some superb group harmonies. Again, it harks back to the nostalgic 'Goin' Back' themes of *Notorious*.

It was written by fellow Buddhist Bob Rafkin, and is a paradoxical take on life on the road and living in the country. Battin had known the song for a long time, and he felt it perfectly conveyed his outlook on life. It's a harmony-drenched Zen ballad that really lifts the album, and for once, it's a decent cover-song choice, with Battin avoiding his quirky novelty song treatments.

As enjoyable as this version is, the original Byrds could've done an even better version the following year – with Clark on lead vocals (he could've even kept the harmonica break-in), and Crosby, McGuinn and Hillman on yearning harmonies.

'Bristol Steam Convention Blues' (Parsons, White)
Bluegrass instrumentals now replaced novelty songs to end Byrds albums. At best, this one is frenzied, with some great banjo from Parsons, who wrote it after missing the convention on two separate visits to Bristol.

It's clearly their riposte to Melchers' treatment of 'Green Apple Quick Step', though it never takes off with any steam (Sorry!), is a tad posturing, and tries to shore up the lack of decent songs. The playing *is* great, though they could've cut a better version if they'd spent more time on it and had an outside producer advising them: a common theme of the album!

The track should've probably been placed elsewhere to raise the tempo on another part of the record, in the same way that 'Green Apple Quick Step' tried to do on *Byrdmaniax*.

It's a closing track that doesn't know whether it's being sincere or is a pastiche.

Connected Flights
'Lost My Drivin' Wheel' (Wiffen)

The following three songs were actually recorded for a possible *Farther Along* follow-up but ended up on McGuinn solo albums or compilations. With the album's lack of McGuinn songs, this seems a very apt song title for this stage of his career.

It was produced by Terry Melcher, who was originally going to produce McGuinn's solo debut, and this version is probably better than his. In fact, this is better than some of the *Farther Along* tracks. McGuinn sings this gentle rocker with conviction, though the vocal is a bit too affected at times, and is a diluted version of Clarence White's nasal whine. Written by David Wiffen, it was later covered by his fellow Canadians, The Cowboy Junkies.

'Born to Rock and Roll' (McGuinn)

This is probably a better version than that on the *Roger McGuinn and Band* album, and it's definitely better than the dreadful version on the *Byrds* reunion album. The song will be discussed in more detail in the next chapter, but here McGuinn adopts a more *straight* vocal compared to the other tongue-in-cheek versions. The arrangement here is more-understated, though the backing vocals – initially sounding otherworldly – become a shriek in the chorus.

'Bag Full of Money' (McGuinn, Levy)

This western waltz also appeared on McGuinn's solo debut, and – again – would've worked better on *Farther Along* than some of the Battin/Fowley songs. But a teasing holler in the instrumental break lets it down, as the break goes nowhere. It also marks the return of McGuinn talking in a song, but this is no 'Chestnut Mare'.

Note that halfway through on the CD reissue, the song stops and starts again with a hidden track: an alternate version of 'Bristol Steam Convention Blues'.

Afterword

The hastily-recorded album failed to halt the band's commercial decline. After the preceding album's post-production excesses, the band were understandably keen to produce themselves with a minimum of fuss but ended up stripping things back too much.

The Byrds toured throughout 1972, but in July, Gene Parsons was fired due to a disagreement over wages. Skip Battin was then dismissed by McGuinn, who persuaded Chris Hillman to briefly rejoin to complete the tour, and they brought in Joe Lala from Manassas to play drums. McGuinn soon disbanded this touring version of the band, as Asylum head David Geffen had the idea to reunite the original lineup.

Byrds (1973)

Personnel:
Jim McGuinn: 12-string guitar, banjo, synthesizer, vocals
Gene Clark: tambourine, guitar, harmonica, vocals
David Crosby: rhythm guitar, vocals
Chris Hillman: bass, guitar, mandolin, vocals
Michael Clarke: drums, congas, percussion
Dallas Taylor: congas, tambourine
Producer: David Crosby
Record label: Asylum
Release date: 7 March 1973
Chart position: UK: 31, US: 20
Running time: 34:54

Why do bands get back together? Unfinished business; a need to revive tired
careers; lucrative financial offers – all of these! When the original Byrds
reformed at McGuinn's house in October 1972, all these factors loomed large.
The Byrds helped create the counterculture, inspired countless bands and
established new rock-music paths. However, this was the first time they'd
played together since Gene Clark left in 1966. McGuinn was playing with two
groups with the same name, as he was still touring with the current Byrds.
Meanwhile, Crosby was on another CSNY hiatus, Hillman was playing with
Manassas, Gene Clark's career had waned commercially, and Michael Clarke
was unemployed.

Asylum's David Geffen offered each original member a lot of money to
record an album. A deal was struck for Crosby and McGuinn to record a duets
album for Columbia in return, though this never happened, as Clive Davis
– who negotiated this with Geffen – was fired from Columbia soon after.
Crosby – then the biggest name – took charge of the sessions. As producer,
he took the CSNY approach rather than the original Byrds' collaborative way,
giving the four distinguished songwriters their own platform to manage their
own material. Crosby's production role meant he also employed some CSNY
session players, such as drummer Dallas Taylor.

In terms of leadership, any Byrds album must have McGuinn as its focus.
But the reunion was all too polite, and lacked the edge and creative tension
that had always helped Byrds sessions in the past. Admittedly, there was also
a lack of focus due to them all being too stoned on Crosby's stronger-than-
average pot!

The *Byrds* album stands up better than *Byrdmaniax* and *Farther Along*,
though it's still only a half-decent, bland 1970s Laurel Canyon rock album.
But it should've been so much more. The band recorded a jazzy version of
'My New Woman', which harked back to the essence of 'Eight Miles High',
but McGuinn held it back for his album. Hillman kept a grasp on 'Lies' for
Manassas, and Crosby held back 'Homeward Through the Haze' and 'Carry

Me' for a mooted CSNY album that never appeared. Imagine those Byrds harmonies on 'Carry Me'! The addition of those tracks would have made *Byrds* more than decent.

This is an obvious example of the superficial nature of the reuniting of some bands. The Byrds' glorious heyday was never going to be replicated, and if anyone was expecting new genres – well, those days were gone. Between 1965 and 1968, The Byrds were a group of diverse talents – not a band put together for Crosby's producer ego trip. This was now a collection of stars placating a reconciliation. If Gary Usher had produced the album (as it had been rumoured), it would've been more than the blandness that resulted, as he would've hopefully persuaded them to use the songs they were keeping for their solo albums.

Also, the band gang mentality is usually impossible to sustain beyond the late-20s – albeit they never had a gang mentality but were more a bunch of creative folkies thrown together for a glorious common cause.

Byrds was released in March 1973 to mixed reviews. It wasn't what was expected of the critics' darlings. The album did manage to reach 31 in the UK and 20 in the US, where it became the band's highest-charting LP (not including *Greatest Hits*) since 1965's *Turn! Turn! Turn!* But critics generally referred to a lack of their signature jangly guitar sound. *Rolling Stone* said that while The Byrds were the most stylistically unified of all American bands, this was an album without style. *Melody Maker* – who'd showered praise on the band's mediocre early-1970s LPs – even admitted that the end product was a pointless exercise. However, the *NME* reckoned that all the old Byrds fans who'd bought it out of duty would've been pleased they weren't being taken for a ride!?

Initially, the band showered each other with compliments – McGuinn swearing the album took off where *Notorious* left off. Crosby agreed, and thought *Byrds* fulfilled what they could've been. But Hillman later called it the blandest album he'd ever heard, and according to Gene Clark, there were also record company pressures, as they expected too much. In the following years, all members were critical of the album, with a general feeling that the material was weak and that sessions had been rushed. Also, McGuinn and Hillman both correctly observed that with the exception of Gene Clark, the band were reluctant to bring in their strongest songs.

The negative reception resulted in the band losing faith in the idea of going on the road, and with a proposed tour forgotten, so was the promise of a Crosby/McGuinn collaboration. Mere nostalgia wasn't enough to sustain a Byrds reunion in an era where Led Zeppelin and Pink Floyd carried more weight than updated folk rock.

The reunion album was bland, as nobody wanted to step on anyone's toes, and there was no real direction and no essence of The Byrds. The album cover was a bit of a lie, too: a tad too harmonious and buddy-ish looking. Also, they look as if they've aged 17 years, let alone seven. No one was at the helm, being a grown-up and making artistic decisions. In retrospect it all seems like there was an ego vendetta going on with Crosby, especially with the submerging of McGuinn's signature guitar sound. Croz did later admit that it would've been much better if they'd concentrated on the songs more.

When the time came to make the album, the band had come full circle. But as recording began, that old problem was already evident: Gene Clark was writing the best material.

'Full Circle' (Clark)

Clark didn't like the initial idea of calling the album *Full Circle*, as he didn't write the song specifically for the album, having originally recorded a more-restrained version for his *Roadmaster* sessions a few years earlier. But this new version was understandably chosen as the first single and is probably the album's best track. This promising opener hints at past magic. It's a buoyant country rocker with lush acoustic guitars, mandolin and CSN-type harmonies. Hillman's mandolin work is particularly impressive. What could go wrong? Prophetically, the single failed to reach the top 100 in the US or the UK.

This version is slightly faster than Clark's earlier take, and his vocal has more grandeur. Its airy country rock feel also has a slight Eagles sound – The Byrds were clearly joining their own lineage – and Crosby's chorus harmonies are glorious.

This track augured well for what followed, but – sadly – the only other tracks to touch this were Clark's other song and one of the Neil Young covers, which Clark also sang.

'Sweet Mary' (McGuinn, Levy)

This yearning folk-flavoured McGuinn song is a slow burner and is modelled on a sea shanty. Those vintage vocal harmonies have matured through the years, if not the nasal lead vocal. It certainly represents a return to his folk days with the stretched-out vocals. Again, Hillman shines on mandolin (the instrument he actually played when lying about playing bass before joining the band), lending the song a longing melancholy.

The McGuinn/Levy song concerned relationship traumas. In fact, McGuinn's wife Dolores thinks the reference to not needing a wife is about her, even though Levy wrote the lyric. (Mind you, he was a trained psychologist, and probably had enough professional insight to write about the guilt and regret of separation.)

'Changing Heart' (Clark)

This Clark song is of a similar vintage vein to 'Full Circle', and it says a lot that his two contributions were sequenced so early into the record. His songs basically transcended the others' material.

While the acoustic guitar and harmonica give a folk framework, the bass line drives the song compared to the other tracks' more-obvious country rock leanings. The Clark and Crosby chorus harmonies are glorious, though it is difficult to hear that nice Rickenbacker at times – presumably, Crosby was making a statement.

The subject matter mirrors Clark's life of fame slowly deserting him, and perhaps could've used a slightly more melancholy arrangement, though the harmonica works well enough. Parallel to his solo work – which always struggled commercially – there's a continuing theme of anguish in Clark's work. Unlike in his melancholy and romantic 1960s ballads, he dealt with post-fame struggles.

This track is one of the album's few genuine highlights. But sadly, the album had already peaked, with the two best songs coming so early. Despite a snippet of the final track, the rest of the album didn't come as close to past glories.

'For Free' (Mitchell)

It was inevitable that there would be a Joni Mitchell song on this album – Crosby was her biggest fan, and she was now regarded as one of the best contemporary songwriters. Crosby performs with enduring confidence, but musically it's fairly lifeless and the harmonies are stunted. The drum part is too militaristic, and there's not enough going on to hide the fact that it's mainly about Crosby's vocals – and as good as they are, the song sounds out of place on a Byrds album. Crosby should've kept this for a Crosby/Nash project.

The Byrds' best covers used to invigorate, but this song is much more suited to a solo rendition, and does appear on Croz's final album *For Free*. They'd have been better adding glistening harmonies and rich instrumentation to, say, Joni's 'For the Roses'. Imagine hearing Crosby's harmonies on that one, with an *If I Could Only Remember My Name* layered harmony arrangement.

'Born To Rock & Roll' (McGuinn)

Author Martin Orkin summed up this recording perfectly in his *Rivals of the Beatles* book: 'There cannot be another track in recorded history which sounded less like someone who was born to rock 'n' roll'.

It brings to mind journalist Lillian Roxon correctly referring to The Byrds as 'Beatle-ised Dylans' all those years back. McGuinn never sounded too comfortable with absolute rock-'n'-roll material, and sounds off-key here. Although – to cut him some slack – there is an element of the song being semi-serious. Surely.

There's a rather tedious acoustic guitar strum throughout, and Clarke tries to give more life with his drum fills, but it's such a hollow and shallow song. The harmony chorus phrase 'rolling and rocking' is particularly lazy, and the lyric is uninspired and cliched. McGuinn later admitted that the song was too stilted, and that he won't be trying another version after including another lifeless re-recording on his third solo album.

'Things Will be Better' (Hillman, Taylor)

McGuinn's 12-string intro makes a decent effort at rekindling some familiar Rickenbacker magic. Though Hillman claims he was holding back his best stuff for his *Slippin' Away* album, this Dallas Taylor co-write could've been one of that album's best tracks.

Probably due to that ringing Rickenbacker intro, this cautionary tale about the rise and fall of stardom was released as a single but failed to dent the charts. Granted, it's no *Younger Than Yesterday* standout, but unlike 'Time Between' – which should've been longer – this short playing time is about right. The bridges have just the right amount of Byrdsian harmonies, and the refrain's simple melody would probably overstay its welcome if it was repeated too often.

Strangely, Dallas Taylor didn't even mention the song in his *Prisoner of Woodstock* autobiography. Maybe he didn't like it much, or maybe he'd just forgotten it.

'Cowgirl in the Sand' (Young)

The two Neil Young covers were included as he had become the 'new Dylan', but this version lacks any great purpose. It was also released as a single in edited form, but didn't chart. Contrary to popular belief, it was Clark – and not Crosby – who selected the Young songs, after they'd all discussed covering Dylan again.

Clark's harmonica playing and vocal are good, with the harmonica especially giving a wistful country feel. Also, the group harmonies are crystalline. But covering a major talent like Young is difficult – it would've been brave for McGuinn to include a guitar break on a Young song since Neil was such a distinguished guitarist in his own right. His original glorious version of this song is over 10 minutes long, and though The Byrds' version is perfectly pleasant, they could've (like the Joni Mitchell cover) chosen something better – 'Cinnamon Girl' perhaps (also from Young's *Everybody Knows This Is Nowhere* album), or a harmony-laden version of 'Only Love Can Break Your Heart' (from Young's *After The Gold Rush*).

This features Crusaders' bassist Wilton Felder and drummer Johnny Barbata, but no Hillman or Clarke, as Crosby didn't like the original band version.

'Long Live the King' (Crosby)

There's a good McGuinn guitar break here, but the rest is undeveloped and a tad hollow. It's really difficult to hear Crosby sing about the improprieties of celebrity without thinking there's something unsubtle and disingenuous lurking there. Generally, the album has a theme of disgruntled fame – which was prevalent in the preening, confessional singer-songwriters of the time. As such, this song serves as a good example of the album in a microcosm. There's a decent-enough acoustic folk song in there, but it's all rather uninspired, and Crosby had much better material in the wings. The subject matter also predicts the reception that the reunion would receive – while enjoying some kudos associated with reforming, the band would soon be knocked off its throne again.

'Borrowing Time' (Hillman, Lala)

Hillman describing his songs as lower-echelon mediocre throwaways didn't really augur well for the album, but the great man did himself a disservice. This effort has a pleasant-enough CSN feel, and though, admittedly, it's a fairly innocuous track, it again has great mandolin work from Hillman. It would've been great if Clarence had played on this – just imagine his elegant bluegrass picking accompanying Hillman's mandolin runs.

It's been suggested that there should've been extra Gene Clark songs on the album, especially if the likes of Hillman were only providing filler. But while Clark deserved to have more songs here, Hillman's were more-worthy of a place than a couple of the covers, McGuinn's 'Born to Rock & Roll' dirge or even Crosby's contributions.

'Laughing' (Crosby)

Ironically, this was written in 1967, at the time Croz was about to *leave* the band. It's a decent-enough version but is ultimately an unnecessary and inferior re-recording of the song from Crosby's 1971 solo album *If I Could Only Remember My Name*.

Written about George Harrison's involvement with the Maharishi, Crosby probably revived it because he'd written it for *Notorious*. Unfortunately, it's unlikely that a Byrds demo of this exists from the Summer of Love.

Here, the 12-string adds a new layer, and Clarke's drumming – with added drama from the stops at the end of each verse – is great. But you can't listen to this without hearing Jerry Garcia's elegiac pedal steel on Crosby's solo album – the new version is pale compared to that version.

Interestingly, Crosby tried an earlier more-echoey version for the new album (similar to his eerie solo version), which would've been interesting to hear, especially with some other Byrd voices on it. There's also a great unreleased take on CSNY's *Deja Vu* reissue, and one wonders if a similar version, with its lovely guitar runs, could've worked better on this reunion album.

'(See the Sky) About to Rain' (Young)

This Neil Young song was a more-interesting choice in that, at this point, it was unreleased by anyone, and it didn't appear on a Young LP until 1974's classic *On The Beach*. This is better than the 'Cowgirl in the Sand' cover. Clark's vocal reading is more earnest, the harmonies are richer and the mandolin break works really well. In fact, the mandolin was the real star of this album.

Reunion albums shouldn't just be about nostalgia, but sometimes you have to give the people what they want. There's a point towards the end of the

Beach Boys fairly perfunctory 2012 comeback album *That's Why God Made The Radio* when those glorious harmonies sound as good as yesteryear: especially on the glorious 'From There to Back Again'. The Byrds did a similar thing here, where near the end, it stops for a second, and those glistening, ethereal guitars and harmonies provided a kaleidoscopic coda: it was 1965 again. The reunion was worth it for that moment alone. It was a glorious way to end the last song the original Byrds lineup would ever release.

Connected Flights
'She's the Kind of Girl' (Clark)
These two tracks aren't strictly contemporaneous of The Byrds' reunion album, but they're tracks the original Byrds all appeared on in 1970 when Gene Clark was compiling his abandoned *Roadmaster* project. The two songs were recorded in 1970 and although they feature all original members, their parts were added piecemeal, as they weren't getting on well enough to be in the studio at the same time.

Though this was recorded for Gene's album, in truth, it would've been one of their finest 1970s recordings had it appeared on any Byrds album. The lead vocal is pure melancholy Clark, and the backing includes some vintage Crosby harmonies (particularly on the middle eight) and glorious McGuinn guitar patterns.

The argument of them working together again at this point was probably redundant since relations were so fractious. But what can't be denied is this song's strength compared to most 1970s Byrds tracks.

Byrdfact: the flute is played by Bud Shank, and is the exact same flute that was used on The Mamas & The Papas' 'California Dreamin'.

'One in a Hundred' (Clark)
This is simply glorious and is a better version than the one on Clark's 1971 *White Light* album. The track almost dwarfs anything the band recorded in the 1970s and is quintessential original Byrds. McGuinn's ringing Rickenbacker is complemented by sumptuous ethereal harmonies and a classic yearning Clark vocal.

Like 'She's the Kind of Girl', this was recorded in 1970 after Jim Dickson (who was producing Gene Clark) reconnected with Hillman and Clarke, who were both now in The Flying Burrito Brothers. According to Dickson, Crosby did such a good job on the harmonies here, that McGuinn returned to the studio to improve his guitar part. Though the five didn't enter the studio together, it was another example of their fractious relationship producing magic. If Crosby had used an old song like 'Laughing', then this glistening song should've also been included on the reunion album. But the writing credits were being levelled-out: that's Crosby's democracy for you.

When McGuinn's ringing Rickenbacker and Clark's pining vocal appear, this prime Byrds song is so good; it carries a certain sadness – this is what could've been achieved had they stayed together. Bear in mind that when this was recorded, the then-current Byrds were about to record *Byrdmaniax*. From the sublime to the ridiculous!

Epilogue

With the release of the reunion album, this most pioneering of bands
had evolved into tame California soft-rock, and the June-1973 release of
McGuinn's eponymous solo album officially marked the end of The Byrds.

Gene Clark was certainly put in his place, as after the album's release, he
was the support act for McGuinn's residency at The Troubadour. A much
sadder footnote followed the anticlimactic reunion when in the early hours of
15 July 1973, Clarence White was loading guitars into a van after a California
concert and was killed by a drunk driver.

For the final word on the failed reunion, it's important to consider that
though *Byrds* is a flawed album, it completes the story of a band without
whom the history of rock would've been much poorer. In that sense, the
album and the band deserve our respect.

Postscript

The Byrds Box Set (1990)

In August 1990, McGuinn, Crosby and Hillman recorded four new tracks in Nashville. Though Clark and Clarke were not involved due to tensions with their touring version of *The Byrds*, it was the first new material under the Byrds name for 17 years.

It's a magnificent – but not flawless – career overview. But why have the bland black front cover and clip art like individual disc covers when celebrating one of the coolest-looking bands of the 1960s? Full of hits, rarities and most of the essential songs, it perhaps only lags on disc 4. McGuinn – who had the final say on the track list – obviously felt generous towards Gram Parsons, but less so to Gene Clark, as songs such as 'Set You Free This Time' were left off. Though the set offered proof of the band's progression, it had too many late-period tracks, and it's less essential now as most of the rare tracks later appeared on CD reissues of the original albums. Here's a brief summary of the four new tracks.

'He Was a Friend of Mine' (Trad: additional lyrics by McGuinn)

This has McGuinn on lead vocal and 12-string, with Hillman on bass, and Hillman and Crosby on backing vocals. It's an unremarkable rework of the song that appeared on *Turn! Turn! Turn!*.

'Paths of Victory' (Dylan)

Dylan's 1963 cast-off was recorded by McGuinn, with Crosby and Hillman on spirited backing vocals. They had to do a Dylan cover, and this is a perfectly-decent uptempo take, showcasing nice harmonies and 12-string, where they combine folk rock and country rock sounds. But it includes an unadventurous instrumental break.

It's impossible not to contemplate the lyric with phrases like 'trails of troubles' and 'roads of battles'. But the Byrds will still fly!

'From a Distance' (Gold)

A song that used to litter many a great Nanci Griffith concert, Hillman's vocal is perfectly reasonable: never stooping to melodrama. The 12-string run throughout is a wise move, and much better than any Melcher-like *Byrdmaniax* strings would've sounded, at least. However, as writer Richie Unterberger once remarked, this is maudlin.

'Love that Never Dies' (McGuinn, Lynch)

McGuinn wrote this new song with drummer Stan Lynch, though Hillman and Crosby don't appear. While not a special return to form, it's good to hear the Rickenbacker again, sounding similar to McGuinn's excellent *Back to Rio* solo album released the following year. But again, there's an unremarkable middle instrumental passage, and McGuinn's vocal lacks conviction.

In truth, nobody rushed to buy the box set because of those four new tracks, but it was great to hear the musicians record again. There are also two songs from the February-1990 Roy Orbison Tribute Concert: predictably 'Turn! Turn! Turn!' and 'Mr. Tambourine Man'. It's great to hear McGuinn, Crosby and Hillman perform again (Dylan joins them for (unmemorable) backing vocals on 'Mr. Tambourine Man' too), but these performances aren't the sort of thing you'd go back and listen to regularly.

Compilations and Live Albums

There are many Byrds compilations and live albums – too many to consider in detail – and there is real variation in quality. All of the non-album tracks that deserve mention have been covered in Connected Flights in this book's main chapters, so there will only be a brief overview of these albums.

Greatest Hits (1967)

This covers two years! This compilation was a critical and commercial success, peaked at 6 in the US, and was the band's highest-charting album there since their debut. It remains their biggest seller. In mid-1960s Byrds tradition, it has a far-out front cover. *Crawdaddy* magazine's Paul Williams called the album an 'essay into rediscovery'. A 1999 reissue added all the missing singles up to 1967.

Preflyte (1969)

This is covered in the *Mr. Tambourine Man* chapter, but bear in mind there are a few versions. Of particular interest is *Preflyte Plus* (2012), which has extra tracks, early David Crosby and Gene Clark solo tracks, and instrumentals of *Preflyte* songs.

History of the Byrds (1973)

Released to coincide with the reformation of the original Byrds, this had interesting packaging that included liner notes by Kim Fowley, and a Pete Frame Byrds family tree.

The Byrds Play Dylan (1979)

As the best artists at covering Dylan, the 2002 re-release of this is better, as it includes more tracks.

Original Singles: 1965-1967, Volume 1 (1980)
Original Singles: 1967-1969, Volume 2 (1982)

These wonderful compilations show how truly innovative and influential the band were over such a brief time period, covering so many genres. They were must-haves in the early-1980s, as they included the mono singles from the band's strongest era, and in the early-1980s, this compilation was the only place you could easily find 'Lady Friend'.

Never Before (1987)

Though uneven, this was an essential *reissue* of tracks recorded between 1965 and 1967. The CD version was much better, as it had seven more tracks. The album was really Gary Usher's idea, and was an eye-opener for Byrdmaniacs who'd never heard these songs before. Some of these outtakes would've made better choices than some official album tracks, but this fails to appreciate the artistic pressures imposed on artists in the mid-1960s, as it was still the age of the single.

In The Beginning (1988)
This contains tracks from the same pre 'Mr. Tambourine Man' era as Preflyte. However, there are some alternative mixes on this album.

Byrd Parts (2000)
Byrd Parts 2 (2003)
These were for purists and are great for pre-Byrds tracks and the band backing efforts by David Hemmings (with The Byrds' trippy decadence present throughout) and Jackie DeShannon. Perhaps some of these should've been on one of the box sets at the expense of filler from the early-1970s.

Live at Fillmore West Feb 1969 (2000)
An okay but not compelling set, this showed how ragged the band could be live. While White definitely adds bluegrass gravitas, the harmonies aren't too appealing. There's a great relaxed take of 'Bad Night at the Whiskey', though.

Sanctuary Vols I-IV (2000/2001/2002)
These are great themed vinyl-only releases of alternate takes from four different eras, with lovely covers and liners.

The Columbia Singles '65-'67 (2002)
A vinyl-only double album with every single released on Columbia.

Mojo Presents ... An Introduction to The Byrds (2003)
With informative liner notes – as you'd expect from the great Sid Griffin – this compilation also has excellent track choices.

Set You Free 1964-1973: Gene Clark in The Byrds (2004)
This was an excellent and long-overdue compilation of Gene Clark's Byrds songs.

Cancelled Flytes (2004)
This superb 7-inch vinyl-only box collects all the singles, with contemporary sleeves which were planned for release – only to be pulled in favour of other releases.

Another Dimension (2005)
Demos and outtakes from the *Fifth Dimension* sessions, on 10-inch double vinyl.

There Is a Season (2006)
This second box set is the better one, as it's more weighted toward the early and mid-period Byrds.

Straight For the Sun (2014)

Here, the announcer asks the audience to really show their appreciation of the band by having a good sit down! From a decent 1971 college radio broadcast.

Boarding House (Live 1978) (2014)

A McGuinn, Clark & Hillman live set with a cameo from David Crosby, but no Mike Clarke.

Byrds Solo and Post-Byrd Years

Some Byrds members had great commercial success after The Byrds, but none surpassed those first six Byrds albums, with the possible exception of Gram Parsons' solo albums.

McGuinn always felt he was judged against The Byrds' achievements. While being proud of the band, he felt it was a paradoxical dilemma. The diminished influence of the latter-day Byrds probably disturbed McGuinn most, due to David Crosby's rising popularity as a member of Crosby, Stills & Nash (& Young). Since the mid-1990s, McGuinn has concentrated on his successful Folk Den project.

Crosby enjoyed huge success with CSN and CSNY and released the wonderful solo album *If I Could Only Remember My Name* in 1971. In the 2010s, he enjoyed a late-career bloom with a host of solo releases.

Hillman went on to have a fruitful career as a member of The Flying Burrito Brothers, including co-writes with Gram Parsons (on the magnificent *Gilded Palace of Sin* (1969)), Manassas and The Desert Rose Band.

Though not shifting large amounts of units, Gene Clark remained a darling of the music press, especially with his 1974 album *No Other*.

Gram Parsons enhanced his reputation with two well-received solo albums (one posthumous). He died from heart failure in September 1973 after suffering an overdose caused by morphine and alcohol. He died two months after Clarence White, whose death was covered in the *Byrds* chapter.

The closest The Byrds came to a permanent reunion, was the McGuinn, Clark & Hillman band in the late-1970s. But again, Clark bailed out to leave McGuinn and Hillman as a duo for a couple of albums.

In the 1980s, Crosby battled drug problems, and the band legend was tarnished by arguments over rights to use the Byrds name. At one point, Michael Clarke toured with a Byrds concoction that had no other original members. In 1991, tragedy struck when Gene Clark was diagnosed with throat cancer and basically drank himself to death. The thought of not being able to sing was too much for him. He died in May 1991, aged 46, from a heart attack. In 1993, Michael Clark died from liver disease. In the 2000s, drummer Kevin Kelley died of natural causes, and bassist Skip Battin passed after suffering from Alzheimer's disease. Sadly, David Crosby passed away just as the first draft of this book was completed.

Former members Gene Parsons and John York remain active and continue to perform and record various musical projects. Since 2001, Parsons has been devoted to his String Bender guitar business, while York has become a pipe-organ builder.

A nice postscript is that The Byrds were inducted into the Rock and Roll Hall of Fame in 1991, and Hillman has always highlighted the fact that the five of them sat together at the awards. Around this time, Crosby started alluding to the fact that McGuinn was about half the group in terms of knowledge and talent, while venerating his ability and vision to arrange a song. And, through the years, McGuinn had the sense to include Byrds songs in his solo sets: as the best songs don't date.

Moreover, McGuinn and Hillman performed together in 2018 (with backing by Marty Stuart) to celebrate the 50th anniversary of the *Sweetheart of the Rodeo* album. They played some Byrds' songs along with all of *Sweetheart*, and talked about its creation.

These Charming Men: The Byrds' Legacy

The Byrds are the sound of subversive history being made, and their wingspan hanging over popular music is so enormous that it's difficult to cover their legacy succinctly. With experiments in folk, jazz, Indian music, electronics and country, it stands as one of the most significant bodies of work in rock history, and few contemporaries can claim to have made such an impact on pop culture.

Steven Van Zandt reckons they will always be the most important American band, since their harmonies transformed rock-'n'-roll and used jazz chords, and that they helped create the new art of rock music. Author Barney Hoskins says The Byrds' impact striated rock history thanks to their stylistic lineage, and that calling them influential is an understatement.

The word Byrdsian emerged in the mid-1970s, describing artists who saw the soaring possibilities of that trademark 12-string Rickenbacker sound – such as Tom Petty, who, on first hearing The Byrds, thought their ethereal sound was from somewhere he'd never been before. A lot of late-1970s power pop also owes a debt to their sound. The Byrds' innovations have echoed through subsequent decades. In the 1980s, bands like The Pretenders and R.E.M. kept the spirit alive. R.E.M.'s Peter Buck, rather than strumming chords, would pick arpeggios in the style immortalised by McGuinn. The Smiths' greatest appeal was being melancholy through Morrissey's lyrics, and euphoric where Johnny Marr used McGuinn's actual 1960s Rickenbacker guitar to give The Smiths a classic-pop sensibility. This new generation of groups used The Byrds' past to set sights on new horizons. The Rickenbacker sound, which had invented folk rock, became a template for indie pop, where bands like Teenage Fanclub and The Go-Betweens continued to demonstrate a Byrds influence.

The Byrds' acid-rock influence also continued through the mid-1980s, when L.A.'s Paisley Underground scene was hugely influenced by the band's forays into psychedelia. American college radio became overrun with US Byrds clones. Bands like The Rain Parade and The Bangles name-dropped the band as a major influence. Husker Du were also Byrds-obsessed in the studio, learning about layering and using backwards effects by listening to them. The lineage continued into the 1990s with bands like Nirvana, whose punk-pop hybrids evoked the spirit of those Byrdsian pop intonations. And the British indie scene continued the renaissance of 1960s pop. The La's' jangly 'There She Goes' owed a drony debt to both The Byrds and The Velvet Underground.

The lineage continued into the 1990s alternative-country movement. Though The Long Ryders are also seen as pioneers in this movement, their leader Sid Griffin always acknowledges the influence of his beloved Byrds, while Wilco's Jeff Tweedy says he learned how to sing harmonies from listening to Byrds records. The alt-country scene has flourished into the 21st century with bands like The Jayhawks and The Sadies, replete with sparkly chords and heavenly harmonies, and bands like Fleet Foxes and The Lemon Twigs continue the lineage with their own restless eclecticism.

Writer Colin Larkin reckons that out of The Byrds' contemporaries, only The Beatles have a repertoire of such diversity and adaptability. Through The Byrds' tradition of uniting musical styles that had no previous affinity for each other, they intrinsically affected pop culture by changing the trajectory of the musical movements that followed.

The Byrds' influence carries on through each new generation. One hundred years from now, we will most likely still be singing their praises via 22nd-century playlists – *hyphen-rock* playlists, obviously!

The Byrds: Always Beyond Today!

Bibliography

Byrds books
Rogan, J., *Requiem for the Timeless Vol 1* (Rogan House, 2011)
Hjort, C., *So You Want to Be a Rock 'n' Roll Star* (Jawbone Press, 2008)
Uncut Byrds Ultimate Music Guide magazine (NME Networks, 2018)

General music books
Orkin, M., *Rivals of The Beatles* (MHO Press, 2020)
Unterberger, R., *Eight Miles High* (Backbeat Books, 2003)
Larkin, C., *Virgin Encyclopedia of Popular Music* (Virgin Books, 1997)

Byrds online resources
Unterberger, R., *Jingle Jangle Mornings* (E-book edition, 2014)
All Music Guide: *allmusic.com*
Byrds lyrics page: *byrdslyrics.de*

On Track series

Allman Brothers Band – Andrew Wild
978-1-78952-252-5
Tori Amos – Lisa Torem 978-1-78952-142-9
Aphex Twin – Beau Waddell 978-1-78952-267-9
Asia – Peter Braidis 978-1-78952-099-6
Badfinger – Robert Day-Webb 978-1-878952-176-4
Barclay James Harvest – Keith and Monica Domone
978-1-78952-067-5
Beck – Arthur Lizie 978-1-78952-258-7
The Beatles – Andrew Wild 978-1-78952-009-5
The Beatles Solo 1969-1980 – Andrew Wild
978-1-78952-030-9
Blue Oyster Cult – Jacob Holm-Lupo
978-1-78952-007-1
Blur – Matt Bishop 978-178952-164-1
Marc Bolan and T.Rex – Peter Gallagher
978-1-78952-124-5
Kate Bush – Bill Thomas 978-1-78952-097-2
Camel – Hamish Kuzminski 978-1-78952-040-8
Captain Beefheart – Opher Goodwin
978-1-78952-235-8
Caravan – Andy Boot 978-1-78952-127-6
Cardiacs – Eric Benac 978-1-78952-131-3
Nick Cave and The Bad Seeds – Dominic Sanderson
978-1-78952-240-2
Eric Clapton Solo – Andrew Wild 978-1-78952-141-2
The Clash – Nick Assirati 978-1-78952-077-4
Elvis Costello and The Attractions – Georg Purvis
978-1-78952-129-0
Crosby, Stills and Nash – Andrew Wild
978-1-78952-039-2
Creedence Clearwater Revival – Tony Thompson
978-178952-237-2
The Damned – Morgan Brown 978-1-78952-136-8
Deep Purple and Rainbow 1968-79 – Steve Pilkington
978-1-78952-002-6
Dire Straits – Andrew Wild 978-1-78952-044-6
The Doors – Tony Thompson 978-1-78952-137-5
Dream Theater – Jordan Blum 978-1-78952-050-7
Eagles – John Van der Kiste 978-1-78952-260-0
Earth, Wind and Fire – Bud Wilkins
978-1-78952-272-9
Electric Light Orchestra – Barry Delve
978-1-78952-152-8
Emerson Lake and Palmer – Mike Goode
978-1-78952-000-2
Fairport Convention – Kevan Furbank
978-1-78952-051-4
Peter Gabriel – Graeme Scarfe 978-1-78952-138-2
Genesis – Stuart MacFarlane 978-1-78952-005-7
Gentle Giant – Gary Steel 978-1-78952-058-3
Gong – Kevan Furbank 978-1-78952-082-8
Green Day – William E. Spevack 978-1-78952-261-7
Hall and Oates – Ian Abrahams 978-1-78952-167-2
Hawkwind – Duncan Harris 978-1-78952-052-1
Peter Hammill – Richard Rees Jones
978-1-78952-163-4
Roy Harper – Opher Goodwin 978-1-78952-130-6
Jimi Hendrix – Emma Stott 978-1-78952-175-7
The Hollies – Andrew Darlington 978-1-78952-159-7
Horslips – Richard James 978-1-78952-263-1
The Human League and The Sheffield Scene –

Andrew Darlington 978-1-78952-186-3
The Incredible String Band – Tim Moon
978-1-78952-107-8
Iron Maiden – Steve Pilkington 978-1-78952-061-3
Joe Jackson – Richard James 978-1-78952-189-4
Jefferson Airplane – Richard Butterworth
978-1-78952-143-6
Jethro Tull – Jordan Blum 978-1-78952-016-3
Elton John in the 1970s – Peter Kearns
978-1-78952-034-7
Billy Joel – Lisa Torem 978-1-78952-183-2
Judas Priest – John Tucker 978-1-78952-018-7
Kansas – Kevin Cummings 978-1-78952-057-6
The Kinks – Martin Hutchinson 978-1-78952-172-6
Korn – Matt Karpe 978-1-78952-153-5
Led Zeppelin – Steve Pilkington 978-1-78952-151-1
Level 42 – Matt Philips 978-1-78952-102-3
Little Feat – Georg Purvis - 978-1-78952-168-9
Aimee Mann – Jez Rowden 978-1-78952-036-1
Joni Mitchell – Peter Kearns 978-1-78952-081-1
The Moody Blues – Geoffrey Feakes
978-1-78952-042-2
Motorhead – Duncan Harris 978-1-78952-173-3
Nektar – Scott Meze – 978-1-78952-257-0
New Order – Dennis Remmer – 978-1-78952-249-5
Nightwish – Simon McMurdo – 978-1-78952-270-9
Laura Nyro – Philip Ward 978-1-78952-182-5
Mike Oldfield – Ryan Yard 978-1-78952-060-6
Opeth – Jordan Blum 978-1-78-952-166-5
Pearl Jam – Ben L. Connor 978-1-78952-188-7
Tom Petty – Richard James 978-1-78952-128-3
Pink Floyd – Richard Butterworth 978-1-78952-242-6
The Police – Pete Braidis 978-1-78952-158-0
Porcupine Tree – Nick Holmes 978-1-78952-144-3
Queen – Andrew Wild 978-1-78952-003-3
Radiohead – William Allen 978-1-78952-149-8
Rancid – Paul Matts 989-1-78952-187-0
Renaissance – David Detmer 978-1-78952-062-0
REO Speedwagon – Jim Romag 978-1-78952-262-4
The Rolling Stones 1963-80 – Steve Pilkington
978-1-78952-017-0
The Smiths and Morrissey – Tommy Gunnarsson
978-1-78952-140-5
Spirit – Rev. Keith A. Gordon – 978-1-78952- 248-8
Stackridge – Alan Draper 978-1-78952-232-7
Status Quo the Frantic Four Years – Richard James
978-1-78952-160-3
Steely Dan – Jez Rowden 978-1-78952-043-9
Steve Hackett – Geoffrey Feakes 978-1-78952-098-9
Tears For Fears – Paul Clark - 978-178952-238-9
Thin Lizzy – Graeme Stroud 978-1-78952-064-4
Tool – Matt Karpe 978-1-78952-234-1
Toto – Jacob Holm-Lupo 978-1-78952-019-4
U2 – Eoghan Lyng 978-1-78952-078-1
UFO – Richard James 978-1-78952-073-6
Van Der Graaf Generator – Dan Coffey
978-1-78952-031-6
Van Halen – Morgan Brown – 9781-78952-256-3
The Who – Geoffrey Feakes 978-1-78952-076-7
Roy Wood and the Move – James R Turner
978-1-78952-008-8
Yes – Stephen Lambe 978-1-78952-001-9
Frank Zappa 1966 to 1979 – Eric Benac

Also available from Sonicbond

978-1-78952-033-0
Warren Zevon – Peter Gallagher 978-1-78952-170-2
10CC – Peter Kearns 978-1-78952-054-5

Decades Series
The Bee Gees in the 1960s – Andrew Mon Hughes et al
978-1-78952-148-1
The Bee Gees in the 1970s – Andrew Mon Hughes et al
978-1-78952-179-5
Black Sabbath in the 1970s – Chris Sutton
978-1-78952-171-9
Britpop – Peter Richard Adams and Matt Pooler
978-1-78952-169-6
Phil Collins in the 1980s – Andrew Wild
978-1-78952-185-6
Alice Cooper in the 1970s – Chris Sutton
978-1-78952-104-7
Alice Cooper in the 1980s – Chris Sutton
978-1-78952-259-4
Curved Air in the 1970s – Laura Shenton
978-1-78952-069-9
Donovan in the 1960s – Jeff Fitzgerald
978-1-78952-233-4
Bob Dylan in the 1980s – Don Klees
978-1-78952-157-3
Brian Eno in the 1970s – Gary Parsons
978-1-78952-239-6
Faith No More in the 1990s – Matt Karpe
978-1-78952-250-1
Fleetwood Mac in the 1970s – Andrew Wild
978-1-78952-105-4
Fleetwood Mac in the 1980s – Don Klees
978-178952-254-9
Focus in the 1970s – Stephen Lambe
978-1-78952-079-8
Free and Bad Company in the 1970s – John Van der
Kiste 978-1-78952-178-8
Genesis in the 1970s – Bill Thomas 978178952-146-7
George Harrison in the 1970s – Eoghan Lyng
978-1-78952-174-0
Kiss in the 1970s – Peter Gallagher 978-1-78952-246-4
Manfred Mann's Earth Band in the 1970s – John Van
der Kiste 978178952-243-3
Marillion in the 1980s – Nathaniel Webb
978-1-78952-065-1
Van Morrison in the 1970s – Peter Childs -
978-1-78952-241-9
Mott the Hoople and Ian Hunter in the 1970s –
John Van der Kiste 978-1-78-952-162-7
Pink Floyd In The 1970s – Georg Purvis
978-1-78952-072-9
Suzi Quatro in the 1970s – Darren Johnson
978-1-78952-236-5
Queen in the 1970s – James Griffiths
978-1-78952-265-5
Roxy Music in the 1970s – Dave Thompson
978-1-78952-180-1
Slade in the 1970s – Darren Johnson
978-1-78952-268-6

Status Quo in the 1980s – Greg Harper
978-1-78952-244-0
Tangerine Dream in the 1970s – Stephen Palmer
978-1-78952-161-0
The Sweet in the 1970s – Darren Johnson
978-1-78952-139-9
Uriah Heep in the 1970s – Steve Pilkington
978-1-78952-103-0
Van der Graaf Generator in the 1970s –
Steve Pilkington 978-1-78952-245-7
Rick Wakeman in the 1970s – Geoffrey Feakes
978-1-78952-264-8
Yes in the 1980s – Stephen Lambe with
David Watkinson 978-1-78952-125-2

On Screen series
Carry On... – Stephen Lambe 978-1-78952-004-0
David Cronenberg – Patrick Chapman
978-1-78952-071-2
Doctor Who: The David Tennant Years – Jamie
Hailstone 978-1-78952-066-8
James Bond – Andrew Wild 978-1-78952-010-1
Monty Python – Steve Pilkington 978-1-78952-047-7
Seinfeld Seasons 1 to 5 – Stephen Lambe
978-1-78952-012-5

Other Books
1967: A Year In Psychedelic Rock 978-1-78952-155-9
1970: A Year In Rock – John Van der Kiste
978-1-78952-147-4
1973: The Golden Year of Progressive Rock
978-1-78952-165-8
Babysitting A Band On The Rocks – G.D. Praetorius
978-1-78952-106-1
Eric Clapton Sessions – Andrew Wild
978-1-78952-177-1
Derek Taylor: For Your Radioactive Children –
Andrew Darlington 978-1-78952-038-5
The Golden Road: The Recording History of The
Grateful Dead – John Kilbride 978-1-78952-156-6
Iggy and The Stooges On Stage 1967-1974 –
Per Nilsen 978-1-78952-101-6
Jon Anderson and the Warriors – the road to Yes –
David Watkinson 978-1-78952-059-0
Magic: The David Paton Story – David Paton
978-1-78952-266-2
Misty: The Music of Johnny Mathis – Jakob Baekgaard
978-1-78952-247-1
Nu Metal: A Definitive Guide – Matt Karpe
978-1-78952-063-7
Tommy Bolin: In and Out of Deep Purple – Laura
Shenton 978-1-78952-070-5
Maximum Darkness – Deke Leonard
978-1-78952-048-4
The Twang Dynasty – Deke Leonard
978-1-78952-049-1

and many more to come!